SIGN LANGUAGE COMPANION

A Handbook of British Signs

CATH SMITH

Illustrated by David Hodgson

A CONDOR BOOK
SOUVENIR PRESS (E&A) LTD

By the same author

SIGNS MAKE SENSE: A Guide to British Sign Language
SIGN IN SIGHT: A Step into the Deaf World

First published 1996 by Souvenir Press (Educational & Academic) Ltd,
43 Great Russell Street, London WC1B 3PA

Reprinted 1996, 1997, 1998 (twice), 1999 (twice), 2000, 2001, 2003, 2004, 2005, 2007, 2010, 2014, 2016

ISBN 978 0 285 63333 9

Typeset by Rowland Phototypesetting, Bury St Edmunds, Suffolk
Printed and bound in India by Replika Press Pvt. Ltd.

CONTENTS

SECTION SEVEN: COLOUR AND TIME AND THIS AND THAT

APPENDICES

ACKNOWLEDGEMENTS

Many, many thanks to:

Beverley School for the Deaf for permission to reproduce a selection of illustrations from the third edition of *Communication Link: a dictionary of signs*.

My Deaf colleagues at the school for sharing their native expertise and knowledge of BSL:
Pauline Hodgson, **Malcolm Haywood**, **Anita Duffy** and **Sandra Teasdale**.

My family, and to **cousin Patricia** in particular for being instrumental in the basic book idea.

And, once again, to **David Hodgson** who has drawn literally thousands of signs over the years, helping us all to keep pace with the living language of BSL.

INTRODUCTION

British Sign Language (BSL) is Britain's fourth language. What are the first three? Some rather inventive suggestions have been given in answer to this question, as wide-ranging as Punjabi, Semaphore and French! Britain's indigenous languages, those that have evolved naturally in this country, are English, Welsh and Scottish Gaelic. (Walk through any big British town and you can hear languages as diverse as Cantonese, Spanish, Urdu and Greek, but these are not native to Britain.)

According to the 1991 census 527,510 people said they spoke Welsh and 69,000 said they spoke Scottish Gaelic (whether they answered in Welsh and Scottish Gaelic is not clear). There was no information in the census to indicate the number of people using BSL, but according to the British Deaf Association there are approximately 62,000 sign language users in Britain.

Mainly due to public pressure, Welsh is increasingly used in schools and public services. There are Welsh radio stations, newspapers and a television channel, S4C. Scottish Gaelic is used in some schools, but speakers have limited legal rights. The Scots language is different from Scottish Gaelic and is often regarded as a northern dialect of English rather than a separate language, although some television interviews use subtitles just in case! Most Scots people speak a mixture of Scots and English, but English is the language of education and government. What of Irish Gaelic? There are speakers of Irish Gaelic in Northern Ireland, but it has no official status there.

In many ways, status (and power) is really what many of the issues concerning language are all about, and people tend to be fiercely precious about their language with its varieties of accents and dialects. This is not surprising since it is so much part of our inner being, reflecting our cultural background and identity.

The situation for BSL users has similarities with other 'minority' language users and also important differences. In 1988 the European Parliament called on member nations to recognise their own sign languages as official languages of their countries, yet BSL is still not fully recognised as a language of Britain. This has implications for its status and the status of the Deaf community who use it, with the result that BSL is not used for teaching in the majority of schools attended by deaf children, is not a language option in mainstream schools, and there are virtually no Deaf* teachers of the deaf (with a very few exceptions). Policies, determined in the main by non-Deaf people, continue to promote speech and lipreading (oral communication), or sign systems that support oral communication but which lack the visual grammar of BSL that gives the unconstrained and natural communication needed for the early development of a first language.

Another fundamental difference concerns bilingualism—a person's ability to use two native or habitual languages. It is very unlikely that speakers of Welsh or Scottish Gaelic will be monolingual—that is, only able to use that language—they will be bilingual in English and the minority language and able to function in both, even if they prefer their own language. They share a stake in the language in power and can be part of the democratic decision-making process; they can make their voices heard. People who are born severely or profoundly deaf, or who become so before the age of two when spoken language is

---

* The convention of the upper case 'D' in *Deaf* refers to people who identify themselves as Deaf community members and sign language users.

starting to emerge, **are not likely to develop English as a natural first language** (again there are exceptions but they are few). Many do not gain competence in English at all. Deaf children are at a huge disadvantage in cases where their degree of deafness is so severe that they cannot acquire the spoken language of the home and society with ease, even with the best amplification. It is not simply that Deaf people choose BSL in preference to English, but that BSL is essential to them: it is their first language even if acquired later than usual for a first language, since few get the opportunity to develop BSL in their early years either. This lack of access to language in the crucial early pre-school years, when language 'happens' to children, cannot be easily or fully made up. Unless special measures are taken, most deaf children will have only the most rudimentary of language skills by the time they reach school age. By contrast, children of the same age who are not deaf can be expected to have native competence in their use of spoken language with all its subtleties and complexities, ready to begin their education through that language. Deaf children need two languages (BSL **and** English) for healthy growth and development and participation in society, but far from having a bilingual option, many deaf children are in danger of having no true language foundations at all.

The usual way that language is acquired by children is through communication with their families and those around them. Scottish Gaelic speakers are found mainly in the Outer Hebrides and, not surprisingly, the people who speak Welsh are mostly found in Wales. They live in homes and communities made up of native users of their language. BSL is not bound by geographical location in the same way since infant deafness occurs randomly throughout the country, roughly at the rate of one per thousand of the population. Even more significantly, it occurs in families who are not themselves deaf (approximately 90 per cent), who are not sign language users, and who probably know nothing about either when they first discover that their child is deaf. The natural and usual way of language being passed from parent to child, which is the norm for spoken language, is only available to the 10 per cent of deaf children born to Deaf sign language users—the most substantial difference of all.

A HEAD FOR LANGUAGE

How the brain works in relation to language has some interesting aspects that are useful to think about. A possible place to start is with the young infant. The word 'infant' itself is derived from Latin and means 'non-speaking'. The period of the brain's greatest plasticity, when it is at its most receptive to language, is from this stage of infancy until about three years of age. This is when children make the most spectacular progress in building their own constructions and producing for themselves a language that has not been 'taught' to them, but has been shared with them. It is this sharing, the everyday meaningful exchanges of family and community, that enables this phenomenon to happen, an ability that diminishes as the child matures. This critical period is the same for all human beings with healthy brains, deaf or hearing. None of us are born with a language but we *are* born with an innate capacity for it. Deaf children may face obstacles to the natural development of language, but they have no inherent lack of ability.

It has been known for some time that the left hemisphere of the brain processes spoken language and that the right side is specialised for visual, spatial tasks. Since sign language is a visual, spatial language, it might be expected that the brain would deal with it in the right hemisphere, but studies have shown that sign language is also processed on the left side. In other words, the brain treats sign language as a language, and deals with it in the same (left) hemisphere as spoken language.

In addition, it is known that humans have a fairly limited ability to remember things that do not in themselves carry meaning and will not be permanently stored—like a telephone number, for example, that we might need to remember just long enough to write down or dial, repeating it over to ourselves to keep it in mind. Numbers longer than eight or nine digits can prove difficult if not impossible to retain in this way. When a message carries meaning, it is the meaning that we take in and remember and not the actual words used. This to some extent regulates our language patterns, organising them in meaningful chunks that can be coped with one bit at a time, since we need to be able to retain the actual words or signs used just long enough to elicit their underlying meaning. Languages have all evolved with their own particular patterns which allow such chunking of meaning in a way wholly suited to that language.

When we converse in our own language, we are thinking and planning our ideas based on their meaning rather than the way we will express them. We just concentrate on what we want to 'say' and the words or signs more or less take care of themselves spontaneously, based on these naturally evolved patterns and structures. This is something that happens without conscious effort, but it is useful to consider at this point, since it leads on to explaining why the visual, spatial structures of sign language grammar are so different from the structures of spoken language, and why this is essential in allowing these natural human processes to happen.

Spoken languages have evolved over thousands and thousands of years. They are particularly suited to the *auditory* medium, expressed by mouth and taken in by the ear. Less is known about sign languages than spoken languages and their study is still fairly new, but it is clear that sign languages have also evolved over time to suit the *visual* medium, expressed by physical movements and taken in by the eye.

Spoken language involves words in sequence, one following another, and lots of them. The grammar affects the order of the words and their combinations, the different beginnings and endings that can be added to them, combined with the way that they are said, to communicate what we mean. Through the ear, the brain processes and decodes this linear information, not all in one go but bit by bit, in small units of meaning—the phrases, clauses and sentences in which it is expressed. If these units are lengthy, meaning may be lost because of the natural limits to this part of our memory and our inability to process a message that is too stretched out. We may find people difficult to understand if they use long and convoluted ideas, jumping from one half-finished concept to the next and generally 'going all round the houses' to explain something, leaving us unsure of their meaning. This does not mean that we fail to understand the words or the phrases or even the concepts being used, but that the overall message or proposition has been lost, leaving us puzzled. Good communicators tend to order and express their thoughts in digestible 'chunks' and are able to adjust these to suit the other person, whatever language they are using.

In sign language, the physical movement of signs is slow compared to the speed of spoken words. Words can be spoken at roughly **double** the rate at which signs can be produced, yet it is possible to interpret from one language to the other in the same space of time without loss of meaning, nuance or intent. How can this be? How can half the number of signs convey the same propositions or ideas as those that might be spoken? The answer is really quite ingenious. Sign language relies less on 'words' and more on the inventive use of space and movement—an alternative and creative visuality, devised by the human brain to fulfil our need for language when the usual channels are not available. It involves the three-dimensional use of space, the location of signs within that space, the speed, direction and type of movement, the handshapes that are used, all combined with non-manual information carried by the head, face and body. All these factors can be taken in by the eye **at the same time**. The order of the message can also be very different, and might involve a completely different starting point, construct of events, and finishing point, not unlike the old story of asking directions and being told, 'If I were going there, I wouldn't start from here.' Things can happen **simultaneously** in a visual language, concentrating detail relevant to the message into the signs in a very economic way, so that the rate of ideas and chunks of meaning remain within the brain's normal limits. Now that really takes some getting your head round!

A simple illustration of these processes would be an instruction such as 'turn right at the traffic lights'. In BSL, *traffic lights* (one sign) would be signed first, followed by *turn right* (one sign). This not only reflects the **real order of events**, a crucial and distinguishing feature of visual language, but uses **classifying handshapes** to indicate lights and vehicle, which are **located in space** with appropriate **directional movement** to suit the context. In this way, information is condensed into just two signs, enabling the expression of an instruction that would require six spoken words. Brilliant. Imagine the possibilities in signed English—*turn . . . right . . . at . . . CRUNCH.*

The reason why it is so important to understand this type of process is that it explains some of the misconceptions about sign language, and why Deaf BSL users find signed forms of English such a strain. Deaf people say that when signs are used to accompany speech, they can understand each item as it appears, but find difficulty taking in the message content as a whole when all the information is expressed in the linear sequence of spoken language. The patterning that enables meaning to be given in chunks is inappropriate to sign language, and has to be 'worked out' by the receiver. In addition, because sign production is slower than speech, unless many items are simply missed out, then the whole thing is slowed down. This has the effect of lengthening the units of meaning that put the message across, making understanding more difficult.

Sign-supported English may suit some deaf people in some situations, but does not meet all the linguistic needs of those deaf from infancy **for whom English is not a first language**. Furthermore, it reflects an insistence on 'normalisation' (they **have to** learn English) rather than valuing a unique difference—and making the difference normal. And why not? Surely we need to be more concerned with understanding and respecting language, and less with trying to control it? It seems that the British public at large in increasing numbers are demonstrating their willingness to do just that. The Council for the Advancement of Communication with Deaf People (CACDP) reports that an impressive 15,619 members of the general public took BSL examinations in 1995. This does not include the thousands more who have taken the time and trouble to learn Deaf people's language—in the home, in the work place and socially.

Experts are still unsure how many languages there are throughout the world. It is strangely comforting that we know so little about one of the most basic human dimensions, even within our 'global village' and its information superhighways. Part of the problem lies in defining what makes up a distinct language, with the result that figures as wide-ranging as 500 and 6,000 have been given as estimates for the number of world languages. It is unlikely that these figures would include sign languages, but it does seem clear that there are more languages in the world than countries.

Sign languages do not have the same national boundaries as spoken languages. For example, in the United Kingdom, British Sign Language with its regional variations and two-handed fingerspelling is used in Scotland, England, Wales and the Protestant Deaf community in Northern Ireland (although many Irish Deaf people are bilingual in British and Irish sign languages). Irish Sign Language is regarded as the language of the Roman Catholic Deaf community in Ireland, and has a one-handed fingerspelling system which is also used by some signers in Catholic Deaf communities in various other regions of Britain, including the West of Scotland, North East and North West of England, and London. The Deaf community of Australia uses a recognisable variety of BSL, as does the New Zealand Deaf community, whilst American Sign Language (ASL) is a different language based historically on French Sign Language. So it is possible that countries using the same spoken language have different sign languages, and that countries with different spoken languages can have the same sign language. Confused? It gets better.

The difference between the most diverse spoken languages is small compared to the difference between spoken and signed language, and possibly explains why sign languages have been dismissed for so long as not being true languages. Although many different sign languages exist throughout the world, identifiable by their own distinctive patterns and signs, they appear to have far more in common with each other than different spoken languages, and Deaf people from different nations, even when coming together for the first time, can quickly establish common ground and understanding.

SIGN LANGUAGE COMPANION

This *Sign Language Companion* offers a basic introduction to the vocabulary, the 'words' of BSL, in topics similar to those found in foreign language text books. It is intended to complement and supplement two other publications—*Signs Make Sense: A Guide to British Sign Language*, which groups signs according to their handshape and location, to give links to their meanings, and *Sign in Sight: A Step Into the Deaf World*, which gives an overview of the different experiences and perspectives that influence Deaf people's lives, and sign vocabulary relevant to these topics. The three books cover quite separate aspects of sign language and the Deaf community. Every effort has been made to avoid duplication of the sign contents, although some exceptions have been necessary to allow each book to stand on its own, since each takes a very different approach to the subject. In combination with the other two books, it is hoped that this publication will interest and motivate young people to learn BSL whilst their young brains are still receptive to language! For those poor older people, whether parents of deaf children or professionals whose language learning abilities may be fossilised, this should provide a useful companion and reference guide, that can be returned to again . . . and again . . . and again . . .

Sign language is not word based in the same way that spoken language is and the signs contained in sign language books and dictionaries are few compared to the number of words in spoken language dictionaries, giving a misleading impression that sign languages might be somehow deficient. *The Dictionary of American Sign Language* contains approximately 3,000 signs, and *The Dictionary of British Sign Language/English* contains in the region of 2,000 signs, compared to 600,000 words in the *Oxford English Dictionary*. But this only tells part of the story, since the fullness and expressiveness of BSL involves the creative work of other factors, the rich visual resources that make sign language so different from spoken language and are essential to learning BSL. A comprehensive introduction to BSL grammar and explanation of 'the productive lexicon; those units of meaning which can be combined productively to create words as required' is given in the British Deaf Association's *Dictionary of BSL/English* and is highly recommended.

Illustrated signs such as those contained in this book are presented in a way similar to words found in a dictionary—that is, static and in isolation. When used in real life, signs can look very different, and meanings can vary, depending on the context in which they appear and on the surrounding language, just as words change in spoken communication. BSL and English are different languages, and rarely have direct single word/sign equivalents. The meaning of each sign is given in bold capitals, and corresponds to one or more of the sign's meanings in the context of the topic in which it appears. Additional meanings are given in capitals after the sign's description, but do not include every possible English word (or part of a word) translation of the sign, or other semantic possibilities. For example, the section 'Family, People and Other Animals' includes a sign that has been given the translation **AUNT, AUNTIE** as its main meaning since this is relevant to the context of the topic, and **BATTERY, ELECTRIC** as additional meanings for the same sign in different contexts.

Non-manual features, involving expressive use of the body, head, face or mouth, play a fundamental role in BSL generally, and are usually context specific. Details are occasionally given of these non-manual elements when they have particular significance to the sign, especially where a change in such features can bring a change in meaning. It should be noted that many signers also make some use of English-related mouth patterns to accompany signs. This practice varies considerably from person to person or can vary in different situations with the same individual.

All languages have infinite capacity for development and all, no matter how 'new' or how limited their geographical distribution, have the same potentials and range of possibilities. Language, being the very substance of communication, is constantly changing. New words/ signs are created as older ones are modified in their form or meaning, or become obsolete altogether, reflecting the way people develop and widen their interests and capabilities. Dictionaries and other resource books on language vocabularies need to be faithful recorders of language use, and keep up with such changes as far as possible. However, all languages have a life of their own and are impossible to tie down for long, if at all. Thus it has been written, 'blessed are the lexicographers, for their task is never ending'.

The signs contained in this book are current and up to date at the time of publication, and contain examples of some, but by no means all, variations. Such variations can be compared to the regional accents and dialects of spoken language, or the simple personal choices we can all make from the diverse and fascinating variety of language at our disposal. A simple task, like choosing words for each topic, inevitably became something of a word association exercise, leading to some unlikely and possibly telling links of ideas that just kept growing and growing. However, as an introductory book it had to stop somewhere, but should provide a basis for exchanging ideas and forming relationships, which will enable students to acquire the language through direct experience. The short puzzles at the end of each section are there to remind us, as all word puzzles do, that language should contain an element of fun and entertainment.

Language also reflects our political history, customs, conventions and the values and character of its people. There are many different ways to approach the learning of a language, and the information concerning BSL given in this Introduction presents some aspects that will hopefully prove interesting, and useful to understanding the importance of BSL in Deaf people's lives.

GUIDE TO CAPTIONS

In this book, signs and fingerspelling are described and drawn as if the person making them is right-handed. Naturally, left-handed people will sign and fingerspell using the left hand as the dominant hand.

The captions are intended to add extra information to explain the movement of the hands which cannot always be shown in a drawing. Where possible, a full description of the sign is given, but in some cases the handshapes may not be given if they are clear from the drawing.

To avoid misunderstandings, and lengthy descriptions, set terms describe:
1 Parts of the hand
2 Common handshapes
3 Directions

PARTS OF THE HAND

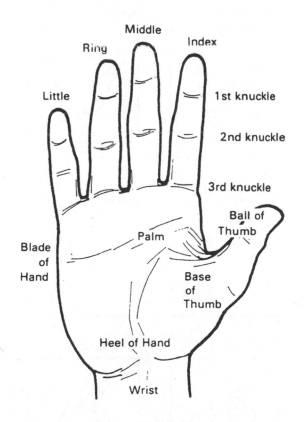

The right hand is always written as R.
The left hand is always written as L.

BASIC HANDSHAPES

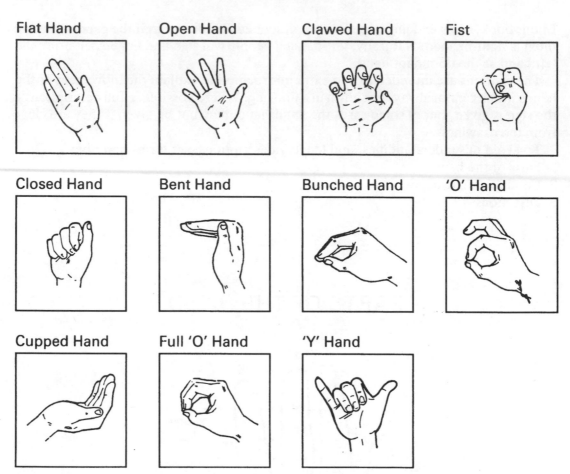

Flat Hand

Open Hand

Clawed Hand

Fist

Closed Hand

Bent Hand

Bunched Hand

'O' Hand

Cupped Hand

Full 'O' Hand

'Y' Hand

Handshapes based on the **Right** handshape of British two-handed fingerspelling.

'C' Hand

Full 'C' Hand

'M' Hand

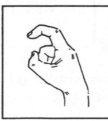

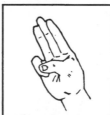

'N' Hand

'R' Hand

'V' Hand

These are the most common handshapes, but do not cover every shape used in BSL. They may be further clarified, e.g. R. hand loosely cupped, L. hand slightly bent, two 'V' hands, fingers bent, etc. If the caption says, e.g. index, middle finger and thumb extended, then it is understood that the other fingers are closed.

DIRECTIONS

The terms used to describe the directions in which the hands are facing, pointing and moving are as follows:

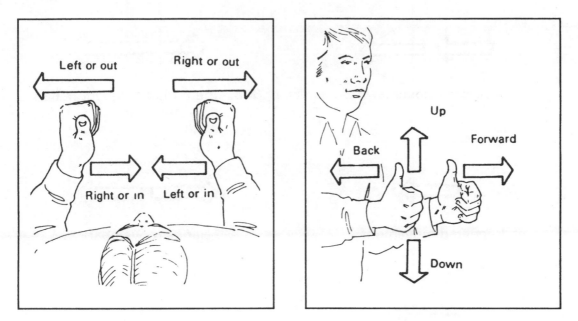

FACING

The direction the palm of the hand faces is given as 'palm up', 'palm back', etc., even if the hand is closed.

In the above illustrations, the R. hand is palm left, the L. hand is palm right. They may also be described as palms facing.

POINTING

The hand may be described as 'pointing' up, forward, etc., even if the fingers are bent in a different direction, or closed.

In the above illustrations, both hands are pointing forward, thumbs up.

MOVEMENT

Where a movement or position is diagonal, it is described as 'forward/left', 'back/right', etc.

Many movements are described as 'hands move alternately'. This means that they move at the same time in opposite directions as in 'up and down', or continuously in the same circular direction, alternately.

Some signs need a full description of handshapes and positions before any movement is made. This is then called a formation, which means they keep their position together as they move.

GUIDE TO DRAWINGS

The following types of arrows mean:

A broke movement.

Movement in one direction then the other.

Repeated movement.

Hands move apart.

The sign ends with stress.

Hands or fingers open then close.

Open hand closes.

Closed hand opens.

Impact on point drawn.

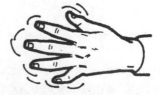

Very small repeated movements.

Hands drawn in dotted lines show the **start** of the sign. Hands drawn in solid lines show the **finish**.

GETTING TO KNOW YOU

HELLO, ALL RIGHT? (GOOD, GREAT)

HELLO

HI

HOW ARE YOU? ARE YOU WELL? (KIND, GENEROUS, FINE, WELL, HEALTH)

DEAF, DEAF PERSON

HEARING, HEARING PERSON

SIGN, SIGN LANGUAGE

CAN, COULD (ABLE, POSSIBLE)

NAME, TO BE CALLED

WHAT? (WHAT FOR?)

I, ME

YOU (HE, HER, HIM, IT, SHE, THAT, THIS)

BELONG TO YOU/HER/HIM/IT (CULTURE)

YOUR, YOURS, YOUR OWN

MINE, MY, MY OWN, BELONG TO ME

OUR, OURS, OUR OWN, BELONG TO US

LIVE, ADDRESS (LIFE, ALIVE, TOILET)

WHERE? WHEREABOUTS? (WHERE FROM?)

NEAR, CLOSE BY, NOT FAR

FAR, LONG WAY AWAY, DISTANT

BRITAIN, BRITISH (HERE, MIDDLESBROUGH, BELFAST)

ENGLAND, ENGLISH

IRELAND, IRISH (POTATO)

SCOTLAND, SCOTTISH

WALES, WELSH

CARDIFF

BRISTOL

BIRMINGHAM

CARLISLE

MANCHESTER

GLASGOW

LONDON (LOUD, NOISE, SOUND)

DUBLIN

LIVERPOOL (LESBIAN, GAY)

BRIGHTON (BELL, GOSH, WOW)

HARTLEPOOL (MONKEY)

AGE, HOW OLD?

11 YEARS OLD, AGED 11

17 YEARS OLD, AGED 17

25 YEARS OLD, AGED 25

SCHOOL

HOME, GO HOME, AT HOME

WORK, JOB, CAREER (OUT OF WORK, UNEMPLOYED)

EXPERIENCE

COLLEGE (UNIVERSITY)

EXAM, TEST

PRACTICE, TRAINING (TRAINEE, STUDENT)

INCOME, BENEFIT, DOLE

MEAN, MEANING

LIPREAD, ORAL (LIPSPEAK, LIP-PATTERN)

FINGERSPELL (British two-handed), SPELL (ONE-HANDED FINGERSPELLING)

SLOW, SLOWLY (LONG TIME, AGES)

SORRY, APOLOGISE, REGRET (MISTAKE)

AGAIN, REPEAT (OFTEN, FREQUENT)

PLEASE

THANK YOU, THANKS, TA (GRATITUDE, GRATEFUL)

Getting to Know You

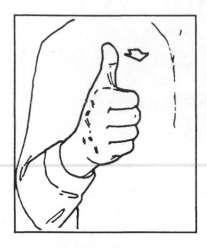

HELLO, ALL RIGHT?
Closed hand with thumb held up makes
small movement forward. Both hands may
be used. **Variation:** open hand palm forward,
pointing up, twists at the wrist, closing to
thumb up palm left. **If the eyebrows are
raised**, the sign produced is ALL RIGHT? As
illustrated, also means: GOOD, GREAT.

HELLO
Palm forward R. open hand moves to right in
small arc.

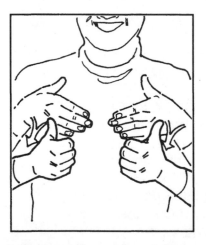

HI
Index edge of bent hand contacts side of
forehead, and makes short movement
forward.

HOW ARE YOU? ARE YOU WELL?
Tips of flat hands contact chest, then move
forward changing to closed hands with
thumbs up. **Raised eyebrows indicate a
question.** One hand may be used. Also
means: KIND, GENEROUS, FINE, WELL,
HEALTH

Getting to Know You

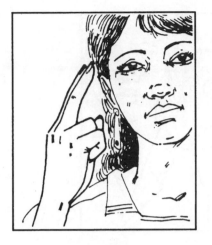

DEAF, DEAF PERSON
Tips of 'N' hand contact ear.

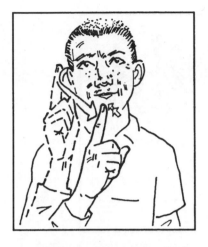

HEARING, HEARING PERSON
Tip of index finger contacts ear then chin.
May tap chin twice. **Variation:** closed hand
with thumb extended; tip of thumb contacts
ear then chin.

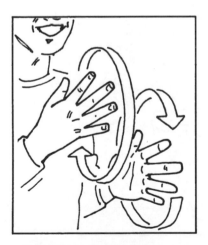

SIGN, SIGN LANGUAGE
Open hands make alternate forward circles.
Can be accompanied by the sign
LANGUAGE (R. open hand palm up on L.
palm moves to the right).

CAN, COULD
'C' hand pointing back in front of nose,
moves forward/down as index flexes.
Sometimes located on forehead. **Variation:**
index and thumb remain straight and close
to touch each other as hand moves forward.
Also means: ABLE, POSSIBLE.

Getting to Know You

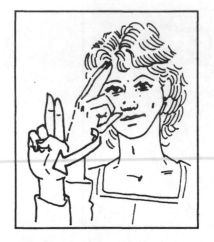

NAME, TO BE CALLED
Tips of 'N' hand contact side of forehead;
hand moves and twists to palm forward.

WHAT?
Index finger points up with palm forward.
Hand shakes from side to side in small quick
movements. **Face and body indicate
question form**. Also means: WHAT FOR?

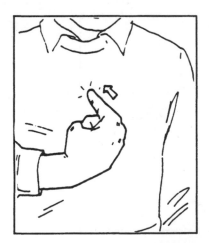

I, ME
Tip of index finger contacts chest.

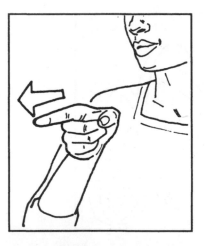

YOU (singular)
Index finger points to person or thing
referred to, accompanied by eye gaze in
same direction. Also means: HE, HER, HIM,
IT, SHE, THAT, THIS. **For plural forms**, index
sweeps sideways in small arc to indicate
persons or things referred to, accompanied
by eye gaze.

Getting to Know You

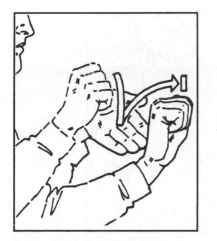

BELONG TO YOU/HER/HIM/IT
R. closed hand palm down contacts L. flat hand, then bounces off and twists forward. Movement can be directed to person or thing referred to, accompanied by eye gaze. Also means: CULTURE.

YOUR, YOURS, YOUR OWN
Palm forward closed hand makes small movement forward to indicate person concerned, accompanied by eye gaze. **For plural forms**, the hand sweeps sideways in small arc.

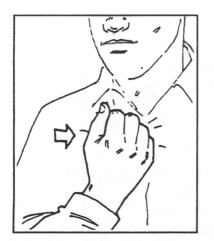

MINE, MY, MY OWN, BELONG TO ME
Closed hand palm back contacts chest. May tap chest twice.

OUR, OURS, OUR OWN, BELONG TO US
Closed hand sweeps round in arc to finish in contact with chest. Both hands can be used simultaneously.

Getting to Know You

LIVE, ADDRESS
Tip of middle finger contacts chest in short repeated up/down movement. A clawed hand can be used. **Variation:** knuckles of closed hand tap twice against cheek (regional). As illustrated, also means: LIFE, ALIVE. TOILET (regional).

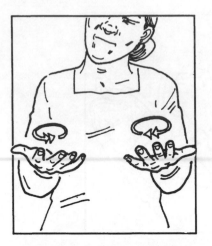

WHERE? WHEREABOUTS?
Palm up open hands make small flat circular movements simultaneously. One hand may be used. **Variation:** palm up flat hand flips over sharply to palm down to mean WHERE FROM? **Face and body indicate question form**.

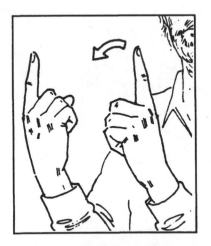

NEAR, CLOSE BY, NOT FAR
Indexes held close together, L. nearest to body. R. hand moves out with small twisting movement. **Variation:** flat hands pointing up, palms facing; R. hand moves in towards L.

FAR, LONG WAY AWAY, DISTANT
Index and thumb extended, hand points forward and makes small quick circular movements, followed by large forward arc with emphasis.

Getting to Know You

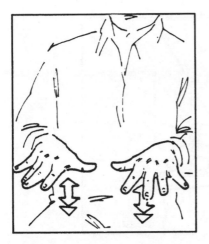

BRITAIN, BRITISH
Palm down open hands make two small downward movements. **Variation:** palm back closed hands brush upwards and contact chest twice simultaneously. As illustrated, also means: HERE, MIDDLESBROUGH (regional), BELFAST (second part of movement moves forward slightly).

ENGLAND, ENGLISH
R. extended index rubs along L. extended index several times.

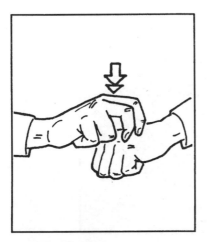

IRELAND, IRISH
Fingertips of R. bent 'V' hand tap back of L. closed hand twice. **Variation:** tip of R. middle finger flexed against thumb tip makes flicking movement on left shoulder. As illustrated, also means: POTATO (regional).

SCOTLAND, SCOTTISH
Elbow moves in and out in repeated movement to contact side of body.

Getting to Know You

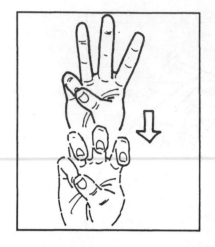

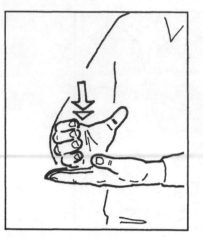

WALES, WELSH
Index, middle and ring fingers extended and open, palm forward; hand makes small movement down as fingers bend.

CARDIFF
R. full 'C' hand taps edge down onto L. palm twice.

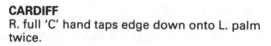
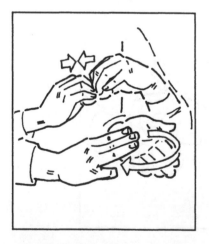

BRISTOL
Fingerspell 'B' 'L'. **Variation**: index and thumb extended from closed hand; thumb flexes.

BIRMINGHAM
Form fingerspelt 'B' formation, then sweep R. hand in circular clockwise motion, ending with fingerspelt 'M' formation. **Variation**: bent hand held near side of face opens and closes thumb onto fingers as hand moves outwards.

Getting to Know You

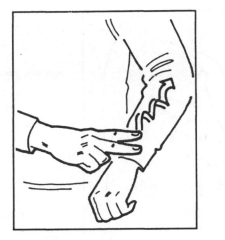

CARLISLE
Palm down R. 'V' hand moves up L. forearm in series of small hops.

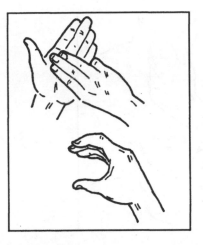

MANCHESTER
Hands form fingerspelt 'M' formation, then R. hand moves up, changing into full 'C' hand. **Variation**: thumb tip of palm back open hand contacts the chin (regional).

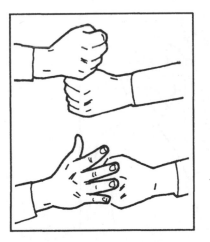

GLASGOW
Hands form fingerspelt 'G' formation, then L. fist contacts palm of R. open hand.

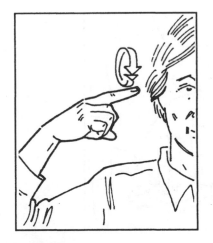

LONDON
Index points to ear and moves in forward circular movement. **Variation**: forearms held forward with bent hands palm down making repeated small downward movement (regional). As illustrated, also means: LOUD, NOISE, SOUND.

Getting to Know You

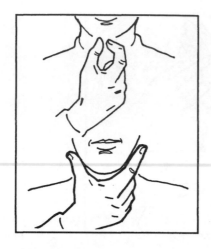

DUBLIN
Tips of index and thumb of palm back closed hand contact chin, then index and thumb open straight and contact chin again.

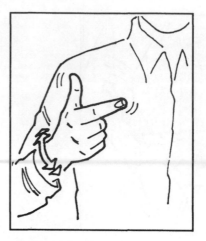

LIVERPOOL
R. index finger and thumb extended; hand makes several short quick twisting movements from the wrist. Also means LESBIAN, and if R. hand is placed on the L. palm, with the same quick twisting movements with the thumb only extended, the meaning is GAY.

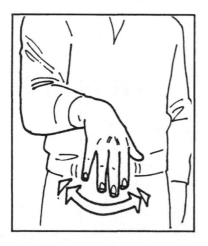

BRIGHTON
Palm back open hand makes quick shaking movement from the wrist. Also means BELL. If the lips are rounded, and eyebrows raised, the meaning can be GOSH, WOW.

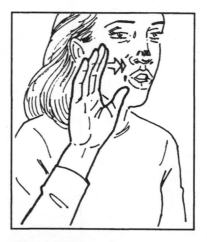

HARTLEPOOL
Index edge of palm forward flat hand brushes forward across the cheek twice (regional). Also means: MONKEY (regional).

Getting to Know You

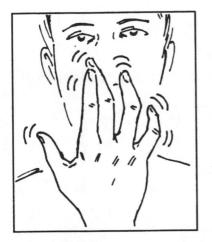

AGE, HOW OLD?
Fingers of palm back open hand flutter in front of nose. **Face and body indicate if question form**.

11 YEARS OLD, AGED 11
Tip of extended thumb contacts nose; hand moves forward/down making small twisting movements from wrist (regional number 11). **Variation**: index extended; tip contacts nose, then hand moves, twisting to palm forward as index closes onto thumb in quick repeated movement (regional 11).

17 YEARS OLD, AGED 17
Extended little and ring fingers contact nose; hand moves forward/down twisting to palm forward as fingers flex twice (regional number 17). **Variation**: index and thumb extended palm back; index contacts nose; hand moves forward/down with small side to side shaking movement (regional 17).

25 YEARS OLD, AGED 25
Palm back 'V' hand moves forward/down from nose, then makes small movement to the right, changing to open hand.

Getting to Know You

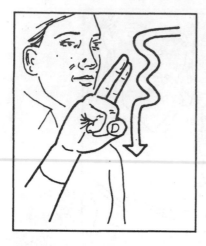

SCHOOL
Palm forward 'N' hand makes sharp side to side movement, as hand moves downwards in front of face. **Variations**: 1. Palm back flat hand makes repeated short side to side movements in front of mouth. 2. Index edge of R. flat hand, palm down, contacts left upper chest twice. (All regional.)

HOME, GO HOME, AT HOME
R. bent hand palm forward twists to palm down as hand moves in forward arc. **Variation**: flat hands (or 'N' hands) held at an angle with fingertips touching, move apart/down.

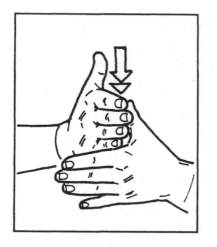

WORK, JOB, CAREER
Blade of R. flat hand chops down twice on index edge of L. flat hand, at right angles. If followed by both hands palm up and moving apart, accompanied by head-shake, the sign produced is OUT OF WORK, UNEMPLOYED.

EXPERIENCE
R. thumb tip contacts side of forehead, then moves down changing to a flat hand with tips brushing down across L. palm.

Getting to Know You

COLLEGE
'C' hand waggles at side of forehead
(regional). **Variation:** indexes held up at
sides of head move in to contact each other
in front of forehead; this version also means
UNIVERSITY.

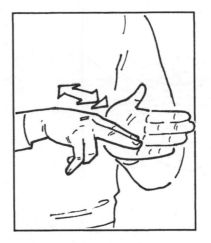

EXAM, TEST
Index edge of R. 'N' hand rubs backwards
and forwards on L. palm. **Variation:** closed
hands palms facing and crossed at the
wrists, R. on L., reverse to L. on R. (regional).

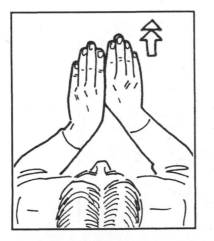

PRACTICE, TRAINING
Index edges of palm down flat hands contact
each other; R. hand brushes forward twice
against L. **Variation:** tips of full 'O' hands
held together; formation makes small
repeated movement backwards and
forwards. This version also means TRAINEE,
STUDENT.

INCOME, BENEFIT, DOLE
Palm up clawed hand makes repeated
movement backward/down to contact side of
body, as the fingers close in a grasping
movement.

Getting to Know You

MEAN, MEANING
Flat hands held palm to palm; R. hand rubs in small circular movements on L. palm.

LIPREAD, ORAL
Palm back 'V' hand with fingers bent makes small circular movement in front of mouth.
Also means: LIPSPEAK, LIP-PATTERN.

FINGERSPELL (British two-handed), SPELL
Finger and thumb tips of bunched hands contact each other with fingers wiggling as formation moves slightly to the right. One hand held palm forward with slight up/down movement and fingers wiggling is used for ONE-HANDED FINGERSPELLING (e.g. American or Irish).

SLOW, SLOWLY
R. flat hand moves slowly up left forearm. R. index finger can alternatively be used. Also means: LONG TIME, AGES.

Getting to Know You

SORRY, APOLOGISE, REGRET
Closed hand rubs in circular movement on chest. **Variations:** 1. Edge of extended little finger contacts chest and hand moves in small circular movements. 2. Palm in clawed hand shakes back and forth at side of head. This version also means MISTAKE.

AGAIN, REPEAT
R. 'V' hand palm left, shakes downwards twice, in quick movements. Also means: OFTEN, FREQUENT.

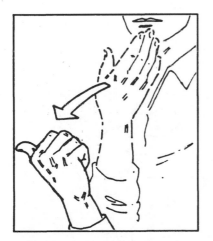

PLEASE
Tips of palm back flat hand contact mouth then hand moves forward/down as fingers close onto palm. Can be made without the final closing movement.

THANK YOU, THANKS, TA
Tips of palm back flat hand contact mouth, then hand swings forward/down to finish palm up. Both hands may be used, moving apart as they swing down. Also means: GRATITUDE, GRATEFUL.

Where are you from?

FAMILY, PEOPLE AND OTHER ANIMALS

FAMILY

HAVE, GOT, POSSESS

BROTHER

SISTER

PARENT(S), MUM AND DAD, MOTHER AND FATHER

DAD, DADDY, FATHER

MUM, MUMMY, MOTHER

BABY, INFANT (DOLL)

DAUGHTER (DAD, DADDY)

SON

GRANDMA, GRANDMOTHER

GRANDAD, GRANDFATHER

AUNT, AUNTIE (BATTERY, ELECTRIC)

UNCLE

COUSIN (SWEDEN, SWEDISH)

HUSBAND, WIFE, SPOUSE (WEDDING, RING)

WOMAN, LADY, FEMALE (FEMININE, ALWAYS)

MAN, GENTLEMAN, MALE (MASCULINE, BEARD)

BOY, LAD (RUSSIA, RUSSIAN, RED)

GIRL, LASS

ADULT, GROWN UP (SECONDARY PUPILS, BIG, TALL)

CHILD, KID (CHILDREN, GROW UP, PRIMARY PUPILS)

YOUNG, YOUTH, YOUNGSTER

OLD, AGED, ELDERLY (DARK, EVENING, NIGHT)

MISTER, MR

MRS

PEOPLE, PUBLIC, HUMAN

CROWD, GROUP OF PEOPLE

PERSON, INDIVIDUAL, STUDENT (PERSONALITY)

SELF, MYSELF, PERSONALLY

YOURSELF, PERSONALLY (HERSELF, HIMSELF, ITSELF)

SOMEONE, ANYONE, WHO? (EVERYONE)

WHO?

STRANGER

FRIEND, PAL, MATE (COLLEAGUE)

NEIGHBOUR, NEXT DOOR

TEACHER, TUTOR, INSTRUCTOR

INTERPRETER, INTERPRET

BOSS, HEAD, CHIEF, PRINCIPAL (AUTHORITY, IN CHARGE)

SUPERVISOR, SUPERVISION (LOOK AFTER, GUARD, CARETAKER)

SOCIAL WORKER

POLICE, POLICE OFFICER

CLERGY, MINISTER, PRIEST, VICAR

DOCTOR

ANIMAL

DOG

CAT

MOUSE

BIRD (DUCK)

FROG, TOAD

RABBIT

SQUIRREL

HORSE

COW

SHEEP (DERBY)

PIG (GREEDY, SELFISH)

Family, People and Other Animals

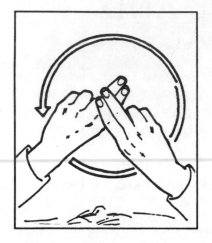

FAMILY
Hands form fingerspelt 'F', then formation moves in small horizontal circle. **Variation**: palm down open hand moves in small horizontal circles.

HAVE, GOT, POSSESS
Clawed hand, palm up, makes short movement down closing sharply to a fist.

BROTHER
Closed hands rub together at second knuckles.

SISTER
Edge of bent index taps twice against nose. **Variation**: bent index contacts nose and hand moves slightly to right with index flicking straight (regional).

Family, People and Other Animals

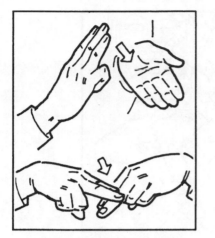

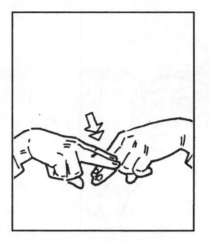

PARENT(S), MUM AND DAD, MOTHER AND FATHER
Fingerspelt 'M' followed by fingerspelt 'F'.

DAD, DADDY, FATHER
Hands in fingerspelt 'F' formation; tap fingers on R. hand twice onto L. **Variation:** a quick repetition of fingerspelt 'D' formation can be used for DAD, DADDY.

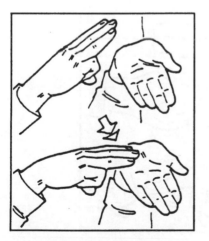

MUM, MUMMY, MOTHER
Tap R. 'M' hand onto L. palm twice. **Variations:** 1. Tips of 'M' hand tap side of forehead twice. 2. R. index taps back of base of L. ring finger twice (both regional).

BABY, INFANT
Arms move from side to side in rocking movement. **Variation:** palm up hands, one on top of the other, move up and down twice. Also means: DOLL.

37

Family, People and Other Animals

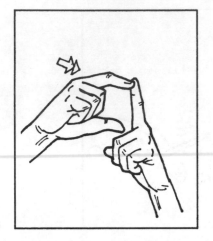

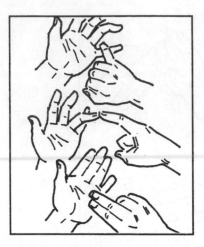

DAUGHTER
Hands form quick repeated fingerspelt 'D' formation. Also means: DAD, DADDY.

SON
'S' 'O' 'N' is fingerspelt rapidly to form a pattern. The sign for 'boy' is also sometimes used.

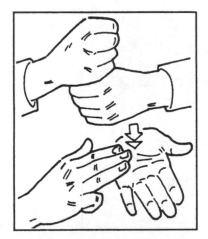

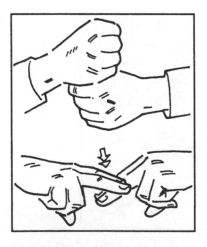

GRANDMA, GRANDMOTHER
Fingerspelt 'G' followed by quick repetition of fingerspelt 'M'.

GRANDAD, GRANDFATHER
Fingerspelt 'G' followed by quick repetition of fingerspelt 'F'.

Family, People and Other Animals

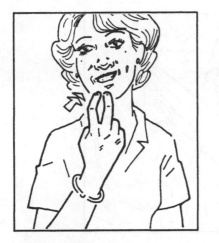

AUNT, AUNTIE
Tips of R. bent 'V' hand tap twice against the chin. **Variation:** tip of R. index taps tip of L. thumb twice. As illustrated, also means: BATTERY, ELECTRIC.

UNCLE
Tip of R. index brushes up/back off tip of extended L. little finger twice. L. hand can be closed as illustrated or all the fingers can be open.

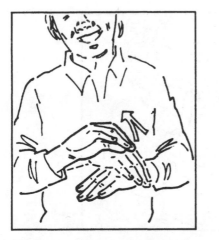

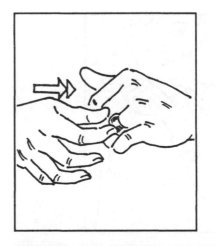

COUSIN
Tips of R. hand hold back of L. wrist, then pull away closing thumb onto fingers. **Variation:** 'C' hand makes small repeated forward movement. As illustrated, also means: SWEDEN, SWEDISH.

HUSBAND, WIFE, SPOUSE
R. thumb and index finger make repeated contact with upper part of L. ring finger. R. thumb and middle finger can alternatively be used. Also means: WEDDING, RING.

Family, People and Other Animals

WOMAN, LADY, FEMALE
Side of index finger brushes forwards across the cheek in small repeated movement. Also means: FEMININE. ALWAYS (regional).

MAN, GENTLEMAN, MALE
Full hand strokes down the chin, closing to a bunched hand. Can be repeated. **Variations:** 1. Index edge of R. full 'C' hand on the chin moves forward/down closing to a fist. 2. Thumb of R. 'L' hand palm back, brushes down right side of chin twice (regional). As illustrated also means: MASCULINE, BEARD.

BOY, LAD
R. index pointing left brushes across the chin in small movement to the left. Can be repeated. **Variations:** 1. Tips of palm back 'N' hand brush down chin twice. 2. Index and thumb make small repeated stroking movement off end of chin. As illustrated, also means: RUSSIA, RUSSIAN. RED (regional).

GIRL, LASS
Side of index finger brushes forwards in small repeated movement near side of mouth. **Variations:** 1. Index tip pointing up brushes right to left across the chin twice. 2. R. index pointing left is drawn left to right across the forehead. (Both regional.)

Family, People and Other Animals

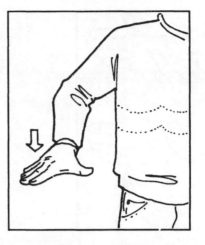

ADULT, GROWN UP
Bent hand makes short movement at head height. In a school context, both hands can be used in small alternate movements to indicate SECONDARY PUPILS. Also means: BIG, TALL.

CHILD, KID
Palm down flat hand makes short downward movement. The movement can be repeated, moving to the right to indicate CHILDREN. (If the hand moves up, the meaning is GROW UP.) In a school context, both hands can move outwards in repeated movement to indicate PRIMARY PUPILS.

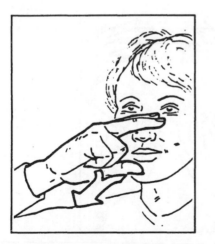

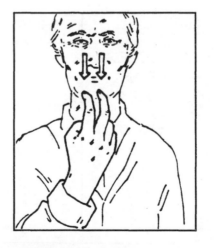

YOUNG, YOUTH, YOUNGSTER
R. index, middle finger and thumb extended; hand moves forward slightly as fingers close onto thumb, in front of nose (regional). **Variation:** hands form fingerspelt 'Y' with R. index making repeated downward brushing movement.

OLD, AGED, ELDERLY
Palm back bent 'V' hand makes small downward movement in front of nose. Also means: DARK, EVENING, NIGHT (regional).

Family, People and Other Animals

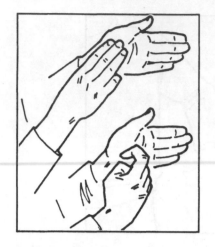

MISTER, MR
Fingerspell 'M' 'R'.

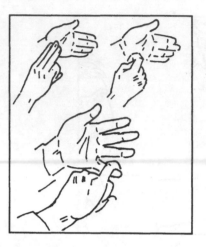

MRS
Fingerspell 'M' 'R' 'S'.

PEOPLE, PUBLIC, HUMAN
Index and thumb stroke down chin, then edge of index brushes forward on cheek.
Variations: 1. Index extended palm forward; hand moves sharply from side to side in downward movement. 2. Full 'O' hand with index and little finger extended; index taps chin twice (both regional).

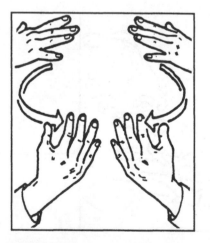

CROWD, GROUP OF PEOPLE
Open hands swing round in horizontal circle.

Family, People and Other Animals

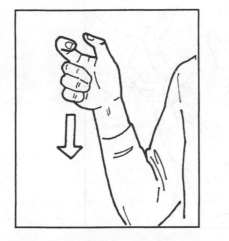

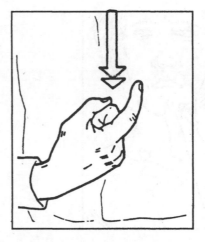

PERSON, INDIVIDUAL, STUDENT
R. 'C' hand palm forward and pointing right, moves down about six inches (15 cm). If the sign is made a number of times side by side in space, it can indicate a number of people or students. Can be turned and made down signer's body to indicate PERSONALITY.

SELF, MYSELF, PERSONALLY
Extended R. index finger, palm right, brushes down the body. Movement can be repeated.

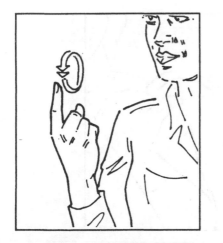

YOURSELF, PERSONALLY
Extended index pointing up, palm back and held forward, makes small repeated downward movement to indicate the person referred to. Also means: HERSELF, HIMSELF, ITSELF. **For plural forms**, both hands can be used in alternate movements.

SOMEONE, ANYONE, WHO?
Extended index pointing up, palm back, moves in small horizontal circles. **Face and body indicate if question form**. If the finger moves in large horizontal circle, the meaning is EVERYONE.

Family, People and Other Animals

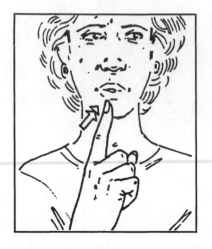

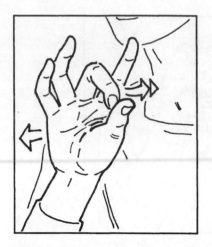

WHO?
Tip of extended R. index taps twice against chin, palm facing left. **Variations:** 1. Edge of bent index contacts chin twice. 2. Index and thumb extended; thumb tip contacts chin as index flexes. (All regional.) **Face and body indicate question form**.

STRANGER
Index tip of palm left R. open hand contacts chin; middle finger flicks out twice off thumb as hand makes short repeated forward movement. **Variation:** index finger moves down from near eye, changing to flat hand, and makes repeated downward movement behind back of L. hand (both regional).

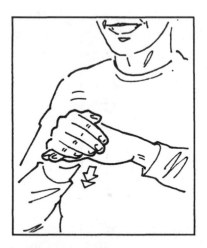

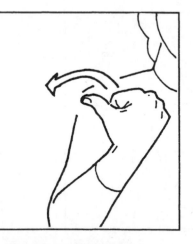

FRIEND, PAL, MATE
Hands are clasped together and make short repeated shaking movement. **Variation:** closed hands with thumbs extended tap together twice or twist against each other (regional). Also means: COLLEAGUE.

NEIGHBOUR, NEXT DOOR
Tip of extended R. thumb contacts shoulder, palm left, then moves out twisting to palm back. May be signed with forward movement. **For plural form**, the movement is repeated several times as the hand moves out to the right, or round in a circle. Both hands may be used.

Family, People and Other Animals

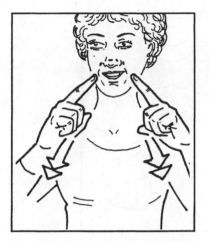

TEACHER, TUTOR, INSTRUCTOR
Indexes extended; hands make two short
movements down and apart from near
mouth. **Variation:** indexes extended, hands
held R. on top of L. at right angles; formation
makes two short downward movements.

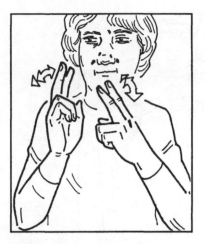

INTERPRETER, INTERPRET
Two 'N' hands make alternate short
backwards and forwards bending
movements from wrists. 'V' hands may
alternatively be used.

BOSS, HEAD, CHIEF, PRINCIPAL
Index extended; hand bends sharply from
wrist to point up at side of head. Movement
may be repeated. Both hands may be used.
Also means: AUTHORITY, IN CHARGE.

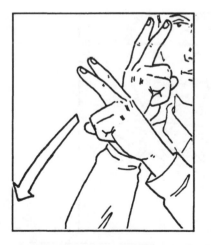

SUPERVISOR, SUPERVISION
Two 'V' hands, R. on top of L. at right angles;
formation moves forward/down from near
eye (directional). Also means: LOOK AFTER,
GUARD, CARETAKER.

Family, People and Other Animals

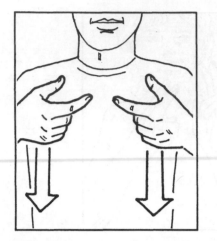

SOCIAL WORKER
Thumb and fingertips of 'C' hands contact sides of upper chest in downward movement. Can be repeated.

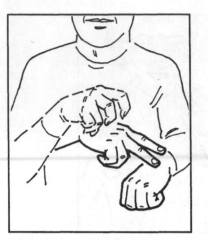

POLICE, POLICE OFFICER
Tips of R. 'V' hand flex as they are drawn along back of L. wrist.

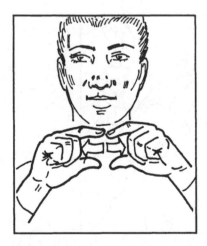

CLERGY, MINISTER, PRIEST, VICAR
Index and thumb tips touch then pull apart round neck. May be signed with one hand.

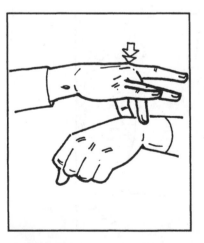

DOCTOR
R. middle finger and thumb tips tap L. wrist twice. Index and thumb tips can be used.

Family, People and Other Animals

ANIMAL
Palm down clawed hands make alternate forward circular clawing movements.

DOG
Two 'N' hands pointing down make two short downward movements. **Variations:** 1. Back of bent hand taps underside of chin. 2. Flat hand taps upper thigh. (Both regional.)

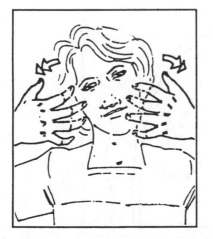

CAT
Open hands at side of face move out slightly flexing to clawed hands in repeated movement. **Variation:** R. flat hand strokes back of L. closed hand (regional).

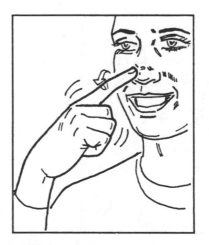

MOUSE
Index twists repeatedly at side of nose.

Family, People and Other Animals

BIRD
Index finger and thumb open and close in front of mouth. If 'N' hand or full hand is used, the sign produced is DUCK.

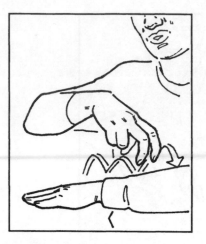

FROG, TOAD
R. 'V' hand pointing down hops up L. forearm, as fingers flex.

RABBIT
Palm forward 'N' hands held at sides of head bend forwards several times.

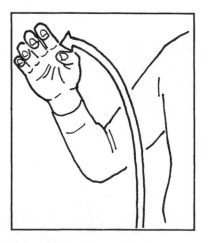

SQUIRREL
Full 'C' hand held at side of waist moves up/out twisting to palm up.

Family, People and Other Animals

HORSE
Closed hands held together make small forward circular movements. **Variation:** two fists, one on top of the other, make small forward circular movements.

COW
Thumbs and little fingers extended held at sides of head; twist from palm down to palm forward. One hand may be used.

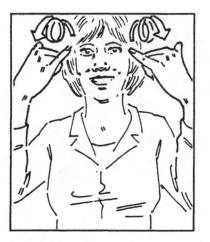

SHEEP
Extended little fingers held at sides of head; hands move forward/down in circular movement. One hand may be used. Also means: DERBY.

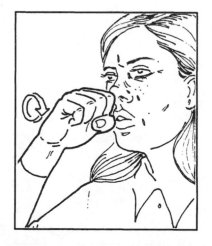

PIG
R. fist moves in small circular movement in front of face. **Variation:** palm back clawed hand held in front of face makes small movement forward (regional). As illustrated, also means: GREEDY, SELFISH.

Who are all these people?

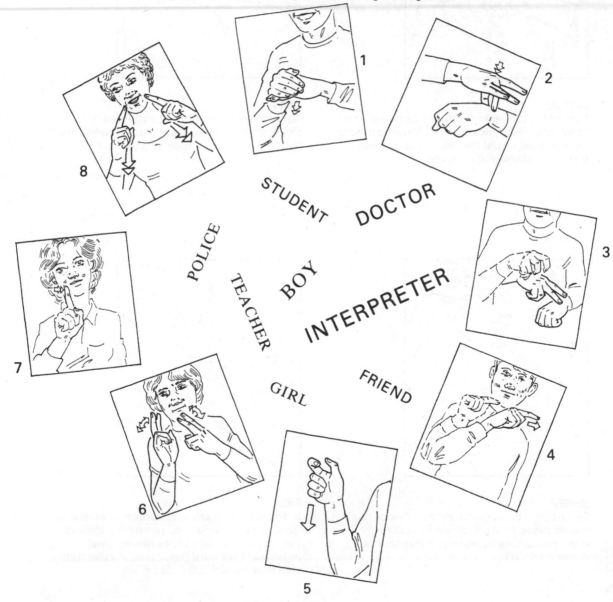

STUDENT

DOCTOR

POLICE

BOY

TEACHER

INTERPRETER

GIRL

FRIEND

Answers: 1 Friend. 2 Doctor. 3 Police. 4 Boy. 5 Student. 6 Interpreter. 7 Girl. 8 Teacher.

CONDUCT AND BEHAVIOUR

BEHAVE, MANNERS, CONDUCT (CALM, PATIENT, TOLERANT)

RUDE, IMPOLITE, BAD-MANNERED

POLITE

CHEEKY, IMPUDENT, INSULT (NAKED, BARE)

READY, PREPARED (ALREADY)

TRY, ATTEMPT, MAKE AN EFFORT (MOST, VERY)

BE QUICK, HURRY UP, QUICKLY

QUIET, QUIETLY, SILENCE

TURN, TAKE TURNS, NEXT (AFTER)

WAIT, HANG ON (SHOP, SHOPPING, LONDON)

EXCUSE ME, PARDON ME (APOLOGISE, FORGIVE)

INTERRUPT, INTERFERE, BUTT IN (ACCESS)

PLAY

GAME

CHEAT

CHECK, INSPECT, TEST

MAYBE, PERHAPS, POSSIBLY

HAPPEN, CROP UP, OCCUR (APPEAR, ARISE)

BAD, AWFUL, TERRIBLE (SEVERE, SERIOUS)

LUCK, LUCKY, GOOD LUCK (CARELESS)

KNOW NOTHING, IGNORANT

EXPLAIN, TELL ABOUT (STORY)

IMPROVE, IMPROVEMENT

BEST

SILLY, DAFT, FOOLISH

SWEAR, CURSE

TELL TALES

IGNORE, TAKE NO NOTICE

ATTITUDE

SHAME, PITY, PATRONISE

PUT UP WITH, TOLERATE

THINK (SENSIBLE)

LIE, FIB

TRUE, TRUST, REAL, SURE (PROMISE, SWEAR, TRUTH)

RIGHT, CORRECT, PROPER

WRONG (WHAT'S THE MATTER? WHAT'S WRONG?)

HELP, AID, ASSIST

GIVE, PASS ON (LET, GIVE PERMISSION)

FAIR, EQUAL (UNEQUAL)

SHARE, SHARE OUT

JOKE, KID, FOOL

SERIOUS, SOLEMN

FUNNY, LAUGH

FUNNY, ODD, STRANGE, WEIRD (STRANGER)

SHY, COY, BASHFUL

TEASE, KID, HAVE ON

CRUEL, MEAN, HURTFUL

BULLY, INTIMIDATE, GET AT

PROVOKE, GOAD, WIND UP

BOTHER, NAUGHTY, TROUBLE (NOT BOTHERED)

BLAME

FAULT

BE CAREFUL, TAKE CARE

HAVE TO, MUST

WHY? REASON

BECAUSE

DANGER, DANGEROUS

HURT, SUFFER, PAINFUL

RISK, RISKY

RESCUE, SAVE, SAFE

ILL, POORLY, SICK (TIRED, WORN OUT)

PREVENT, PROTECT, AVOID

ACCIDENT (MISTAKE)

ALARM, ELECTRIC BELL

LOOK AFTER, CARE FOR (REMEMBER, KEEP IN MIND, KEEP)

DOESN'T MATTER, DON'T CARE

RESPECT, OBEY, HONOUR

DUTY, RESPONSIBILITY

Conduct and Behaviour

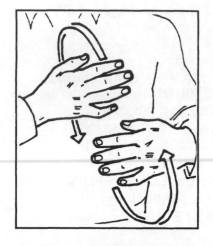

BEHAVE, MANNERS, CONDUCT
Palm back flat hands brush alternately down body in backward circular movement. Also means: CALM, PATIENT, TOLERANT (if the head is down and the lips pressed together).

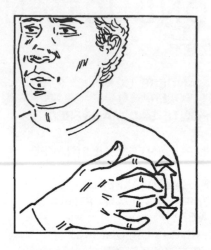

RUDE, IMPOLITE, BAD-MANNERED
Tips of R. clawed hand rub up and down left upper arm or chest.

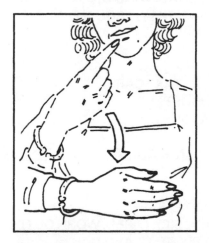

POLITE
Index points to mouth, then hand moves down opening to flat hand brushing down the body (regional).

CHEEKY, IMPUDENT, INSULT
Grasp cheek with bent index and thumb with slight shaking movement. Also means: NAKED, BARE.

Conduct and Behaviour

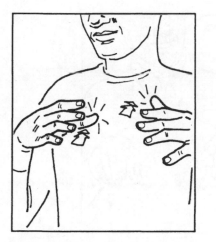

READY, PREPARED
Thumbs of open hands, palm down, tap upper chest twice. May be made with upward movement. One hand may be used. Also means: ALREADY.

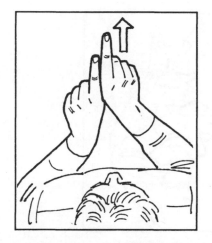

TRY, ATTEMPT, MAKE AN EFFORT
Indexes pointing forward; R. moves forward, brushing against L. Movement can be repeated. Also means: MOST, VERY (if R. index brushes forward against L. in one sharp movement).

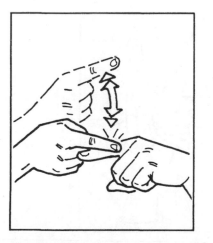

BE QUICK, HURRY UP, QUICKLY
R. index taps on L. several times very quickly.

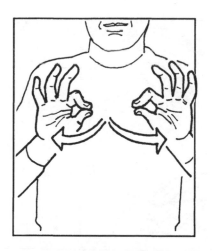

QUIET, QUIETLY, SILENCE
Tips of palm forward 'O' hands contact each other; hands pull slowly apart and down. Can start with open hands crossed, with index and thumbs slowly closing to 'O' hands as hands pull apart. Can be preceded by index held against lips.

Conduct and Behaviour

TURN, TAKE TURNS, NEXT
Closed hand with thumb extended; hand
twists from palm down to palm up in the
direction of the person or object referred to.
Sign can be repeated in horizontal arc to
indicate a group of people. Also means:
AFTER.

WAIT, HANG ON
Palm down bent hands make two small
movements down. Can be signed using
closed hands. **Variation:** palm forward flat
hand held up. As illustrated, also means:
SHOP, SHOPPING, LONDON (regional).

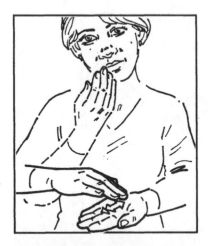

EXCUSE ME, PARDON ME
Tips of flat hand touch lips then make small
side to side rubbing movement on L. palm.
When made with circular rubbing
movement, can mean APOLOGISE,
FORGIVE.

INTERRUPT, INTERFERE, BUTT IN
Fingers of R. hand prod sharply through
fingers of L. hand, in the direction
appropriate to the context, e.g. forwards in
'May I interrupt?' or backwards in 'Please
don't interrupt!' and so on. Also means:
ACCESS.

Conduct and Behaviour

PLAY
Palm up flat hands move simultaneously up/apart in small vertical circles.

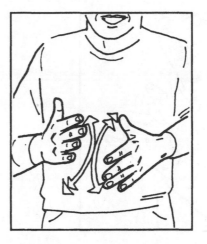

GAME
Palm together open hands brush together in repeated up and down alternate movement. **Variation:** edge of R. fist contacts top of L. fist twice.

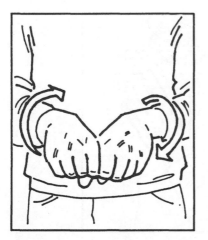

CHEAT
Two fists held together twist against each other. **Variation:** tip of extended thumb moves down cheek.

CHECK, INSPECT, TEST
'Y' hands move down from near face in small alternate twisting movements from the wrist. One hand may be used.

Conduct and Behaviour

MAYBE, PERHAPS, POSSIBLY
Palm left closed hand with thumb and little finger extended makes quick twisting movements from the wrist. **Variation:** palm up flat hands move up and down alternately.

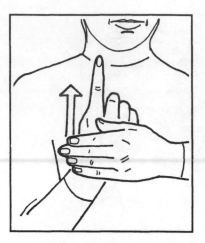

HAPPEN, CROP UP, OCCUR
R. extended index moves sharply upwards behind palm back L. hand. Sometimes made with index flicking upwards in front of L. hand. Also means: APPEAR, ARISE.

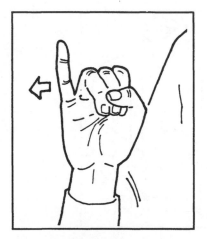

BAD, AWFUL, TERRIBLE
Extended little finger is held pointing up with small forward movement. Can be made with short repeated movement from side to side. Both hands may be used. **Face and body indicate negative form.** Also means: SEVERE, SERIOUS.

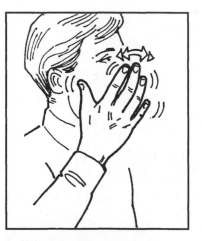

LUCK, LUCKY, GOOD LUCK
Open hand near side of chin makes small shaking movement from wrist (regional). Both hands can be used. **Variation:** index and thumb extended; thumb tip brushes off nose as hand twists sharply at wrist to palm down. As illustrated, also means: CARELESS (the tongue protrudes between the teeth).

Conduct and Behaviour

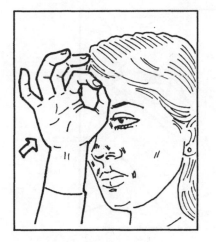

KNOW NOTHING, IGNORANT
Palm left R. 'O' hand held on forehead.

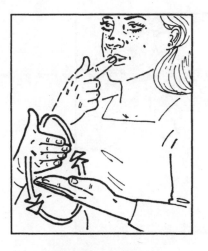

EXPLAIN, TELL ABOUT
Flat hands palm up/back rotate round each other in alternate forward circles. Sign may start with index moving from near the mouth. The hands rotate backwards towards signer in contexts such as 'tell me about it'. Also means: STORY.

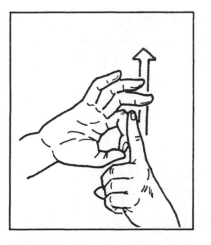

IMPROVE, IMPROVEMENT
Tips of R. 'O' hand move up extended L. index finger.

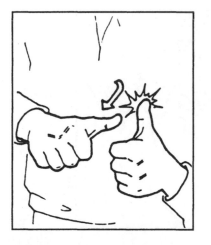

BEST
R. thumb strikes tip of L. thumb in single emphatic forward movement.

Conduct and Behaviour

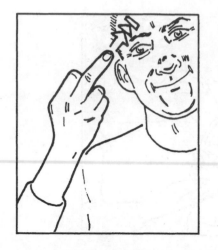

SILLY, DAFT, FOOLISH
Tip of extended middle finger taps forehead twice. The finger may move back towards head without contact. The lips may be stretched and the nose wrinkled.

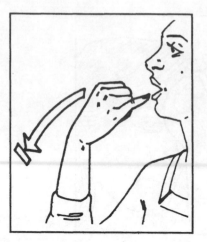

SWEAR, CURSE
Extended little finger moves forward/down from mouth with emphasis. The brows may be furrowed. This sign is used for a variety of swear words.

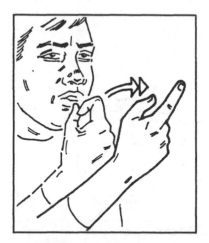

TELL TALES
Bent index finger flicks up sharply in quick repeated movement in front of mouth. The nose may be wrinkled.

IGNORE, TAKE NO NOTICE
Hands palm forward with indexes extended and pointing to ears; hands flick sharply down/sideways. One hand may be used. Hand may twist down/back to contact body as in 'ignore me'.

Conduct and Behaviour

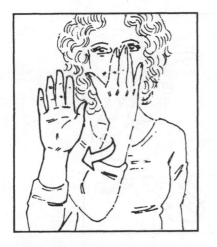

ATTITUDE
Flat hand palm back in front of face moves
forward and twists to palm forward.

SHAME, PITY, PATRONISE
Palm down flat hand moves in repeated
forward/down circular movement.

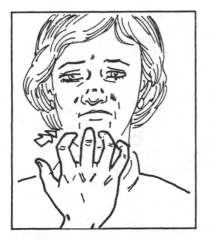

PUT UP WITH, TOLERATE
Fingertips of palm back clawed hand tap
chin several times. The lips may be
stretched. The face and body express
resignation.

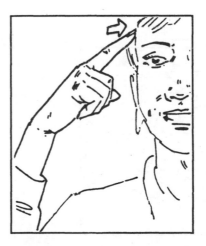

THINK
Tip of extended index finger contacts side of
forehead. A small circular movement may be
used. Repeated tapping of index on forehead
can be used for SENSIBLE.

Conduct and Behaviour

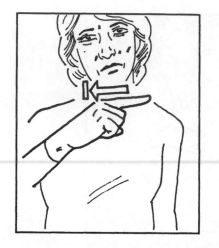

LIE, FIB
Edge of R. index pointing left moves sharply to the right, rubbing across the chin.

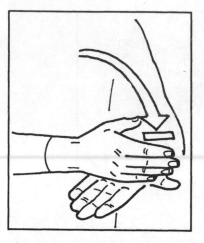

TRUE, TRUST, REAL, SURE
Blade of R. flat hand strikes L. palm with emphasis. Can be second part of a compound sign that starts with index pointing to lips, meaning PROMISE, SWEAR, TRUTH.

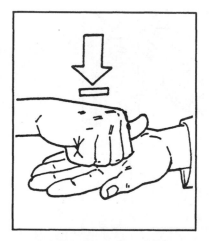

RIGHT, CORRECT, PROPER
Palm down R. closed hand with thumb extended bangs L. palm with emphasis. May contact chest as in 'I'm right' or move and face forward as in 'you're right' and so on.

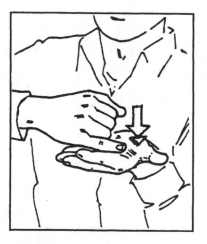

WRONG
Edge of extended little finger contacts the L. palm twice. If the eyebrows are raised, the sign produced is WHAT'S THE MATTER, WHAT'S WRONG. May contact chest as in 'I'm wrong', or move forward as in 'you're wrong' and so on.

Conduct and Behaviour

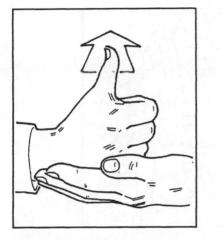

HELP, AID, ASSIST
Edge of R. closed hand rests on L. palm; formation moves in the direction appropriate to the context, e.g. forwards in 'I'll help' or backwards in 'help me' and so on.

GIVE, PASS ON
Palm up flat hands move in the direction appropriate to the context, e.g. forward in small arc in 'I gave' or backwards in 'give me' and so on. One hand may be used. Handshape may vary in context relevant to object being handled. As illustrated, also means: LET, GIVE PERMISSION.

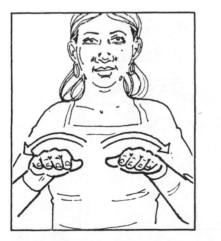

FAIR, EQUAL
Palm down flat hands move apart in small arc (UNEQUAL can be indicated by hands being held at different heights). Sign can be made with hands held R. in front of L. both pointing out; R. moves forward and L. back as in 'we're equal'.

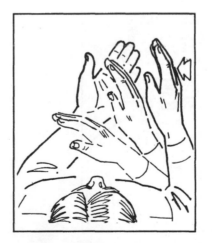

SHARE, SHARE OUT
Blade of R. flat hand chops down along L. palm whilst moving and twisting to point forward. **Variation:** blade of R. hand rests on L. palm; formation makes small movement backwards and forwards.

Conduct and Behaviour

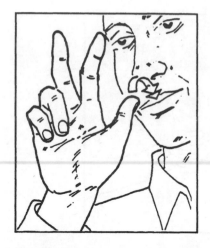

JOKE, KID, FOOL
Index, middle finger and thumb extended and pointing up; thumb tip contacts end of nose in small brushing movements (regional). **Variation**: palm down R. 'V' hand brushes forwards several times along L. index (directional).

SERIOUS, SOLEMN
Palm left R. flat hand moves down in front of nose.

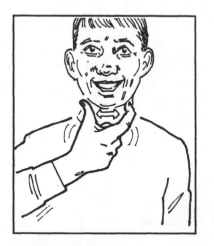

FUNNY, LAUGH
Index and thumb extended and bent; hand makes small side to side movement near chin. Two hands can be used in alternate movement, L. held under R.

FUNNY, ODD, STRANGE, WEIRD
Index flexed on ball of thumb at side of chin flicks out across chin. Also means: STRANGER (regional).

Conduct and Behaviour

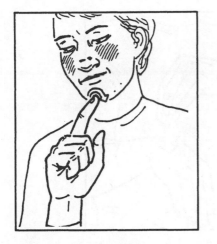

SHY, COY, BASHFUL
Tip of R. index contacts chin and twists from palm left to palm back. The head tilts to one side.

TEASE, KID, HAVE ON
R. open hand brushes forward twice along L. index towards the person being referred to as in 'teasing you' or hands twist to point back with backward movement as in 'teasing me' and so on.

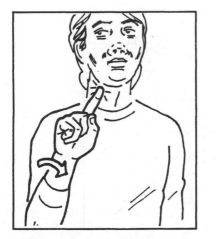

CRUEL, MEAN, HURTFUL
Index tip of palm forward R. hand contacts side of neck; hand twists firmly to palm back.

BULLY, INTIMIDATE, GET AT
Indexes extended and pointing forward make two short forward movements simultaneously, as in 'getting at you', or hands twist to point back with backward movement as in 'bullying me' and so on.

Conduct and Behaviour

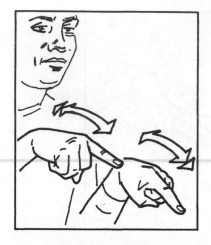

PROVOKE, GOAD, WIND UP
Indexes extended and pointing forward; hands move alternately in short firm movements, forward/down as in 'winding you up' or hands twist to point back with backward movement as in 'goading me' and so on.

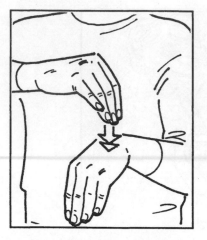

BOTHER, NAUGHTY, TROUBLE
Tips of R. bent hand tap back of L. hand twice. For NOT BOTHERED the R. hand taps the L. hand once, then moves forward twisting to palm up.

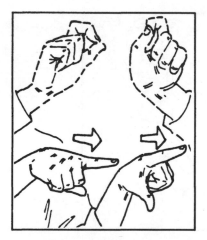

BLAME
Indexes flick out as hands move forward slightly with stress, as in 'blamed you', or hands twist to point back with backward movement as in 'blaming me' and so on.

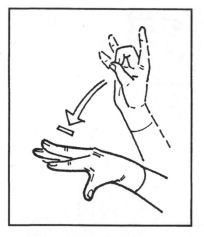

FAULT
Middle finger flexed on ball of thumb, palm forward; hand moves sharply forward/down as finger flicks out as in 'your fault' or hand faces and moves backwards to contact signer as in 'my fault' and so on (regional).

Conduct and Behaviour

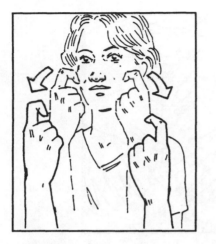

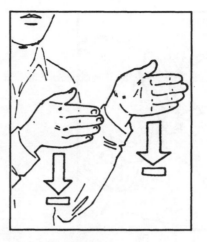

BE CAREFUL, TAKE CARE
Index held under eyes; index fingers flex as hands move forward/down.

HAVE TO, MUST
Palm facing flat hands held apart move sharply down with stress.

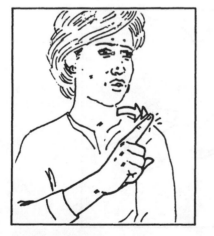

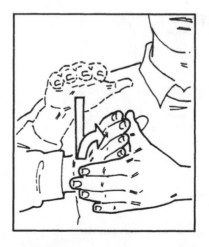

WHY? REASON
Edge of extended R. index taps left shoulder twice. **Face and body indicate if question form**.

BECAUSE
L. flat hand with thumb extended; fingers of R. flat hand contact index edge of L. hand, then R. hand twists and taps against inside edge of L. thumb.

Conduct and Behaviour

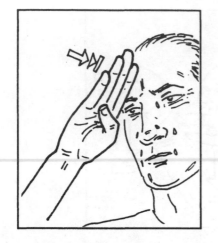

DANGER, DANGEROUS
Palm left R. flat hand moves up sharply so that the side of the index finger contacts the forehead. Contact may be repeated.

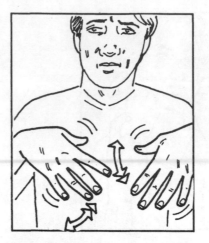

HURT, SUFFER, PAINFUL
Two open hands shake up and down alternately. One hand may be used. **Face and body indicate negative form.**

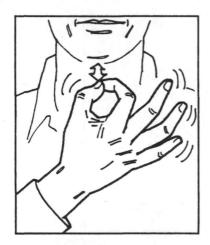

RISK, RISKY
Tips of 'O' hand tap into neck several times in small quick movement.

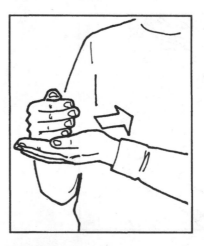

RESCUE, SAVE, SAFE
Blade of R. cupped hand rests on L. palm; formation moves back towards signer.

Conduct and Behaviour

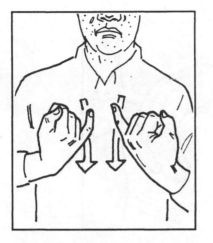

ILL, POORLY, SICK
Edges of extended little fingers brush down body simultaneously. Movement may be repeated. A single slower movement is used to mean TIRED, WORN OUT.

PREVENT, PROTECT, AVOID
R. closed hand pushes forward against L. index with stress.

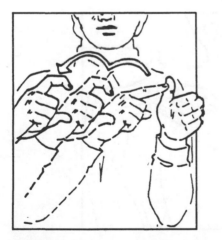

ACCIDENT
Fingerspell 'A', then form letter 'C' and move 'C' hand away to the right in two hops.
Variations: 1. Clawed hand palm in shakes backwards and forwards at side of head. This version also means MISTAKE. 2. Two fists pointing in bang into each other, or R. fist bangs into L. palm.

ALARM, ELECTRIC BELL
The side of extended R. index taps the left palm twice.

Conduct and Behaviour

LOOK AFTER, CARE FOR
R. index moves down from near eye; hand changes to bent hand and taps L. bent hand twice. If the sign starts with index moving down from forehead, the meaning is REMEMBER, KEEP IN MIND. The second part of the sign alone means KEEP.

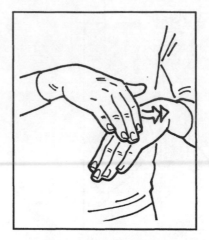

DOESN'T MATTER, DON'T CARE
Tips of R. bent hand contact back of L. hand in repeated forward brushing movement, accompanied by head shake.

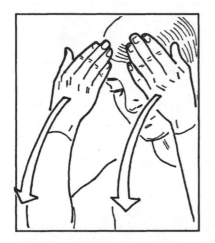

RESPECT, OBEY, HONOUR
Tips of flat hands contact forehead, then drop down and apart, finishing palm up, head slightly bent.

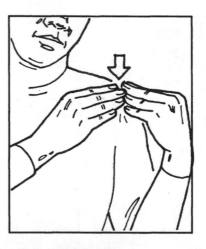

DUTY, RESPONSIBILITY
Tips of two bent hands move down to contact left shoulder. Two 'N' hands may alternatively be used. Hands sometimes overlap.

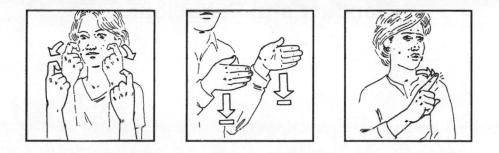

Why do you have to be careful?

DANGER

RISKY

HURT

LOOK AFTER

ILL

SAFE

ACCIDENT

BECAUSE

Answers: 1 Because, 2 Danger, 3 Hurt, 4 Risky, 5 Safe, 6 Ill, 7 Accident, 8 Look after.

69

SHARING IDEAS AND INTERESTS

KNOW, KNOWLEDGE
DON'T KNOW
UNDERSTAND, REALISE, IDEA (AWARE, AWARENESS)
DON'T UNDERSTAND, OVER MY HEAD
BORED, BORING, TEDIOUS, DULL
EXCITED, INTEREST, INTERESTING (EAGER, KEEN, TOILET)
ENJOY, HAPPY, PLEASURE
LEISURE, SPARE TIME, HOLIDAY
LIKE, FOND OF (FRONT)
CAN'T STAND, DETEST, HATE
SUPPORT, SUPPORTER (ENCOURAGE)
FAVOURITE, PREFERENCE
SAME, SIMILAR (ALSO, TOO, LIKE)
DIFFERENT, DIFFERENCE
EASY, SIMPLE (DEAD EASY, DODDLE, SOFT)
HARD, DIFFICULT, PROBLEM (HARD, FIRM)
WISH, DESIRE, FANCY (DRY, THIRSTY)
HOPE (NATIONAL LOTTERY)
WIN, SUCCEED, ACHIEVE
LOSE, DROP (WASTE)
SPORT, ATHLETICS
COMPETITION, FIXTURES
BOTTOM
TOP, IMPORTANT
CANCEL, CALL OFF
SCORE, RESULTS (MATHS)
FOOTBALL
CRICKET
RUGBY
SWIM, BREAST-STROKE (CRAWL)
TENNIS
BADMINTON
ANGLING, FISHING
DANCE, DANCING
RETIRE, RETIREMENT
BREAK, REST, RELAX
HOLIDAY

CAMP, CAMPING, TENT
CARAVAN
HOTEL (HOLIDAY, RESIDENTIAL, STAY OVER)
SPRING (GROW, DEVELOP)
SUMMER (STRANGER)
AUTUMN
WINTER, COLD
RAIN, RAINING (HEAVY RAIN, DOWNPOUR, SNOW, SNOWFALL)
SUN, SUNNY, SUNSHINE (LIGHT, LIGHT ON, LIGHT OFF)
WIND, WINDY
WHICH? EITHER (BETWEEN)
HOT, HEAT (WARM)
GARDEN
FLOWER
DEAD, DIE (DYING)
CELEBRATE, PARTY, HAVE FUN, SOCIAL
EASTER, EASTER EGG
BIRTHDAY
CHRISTMAS
WEEKEND
BABYSIT, SITTER (CHILDCARE, CHILDMINDER)
PUB, BAR
DEAF CLUB (CLUB)
CHURCH, CHAPEL
CAR (DRIVE)
BOOK, CATALOGUE
COMPUTER (COMPUTER KEYBOARD)
SHOP (NEW YORK)
LOOK AROUND, SIGHTSEEING, TOUR (LOOK)
VIDEO
HIRE, BORROW (LEND)
TV, TELEVISION, TELLY (MONITOR, SCREEN)
CINEMA, TV PROGRAMME
COMIC, MAGAZINE (NEWSPAPER)
NEWS

Sharing Ideas and Interests

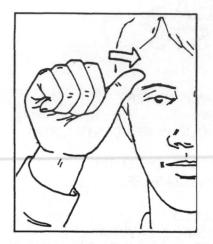

KNOW, KNOWLEDGE
Tip of extended thumb contacts side of forehead.

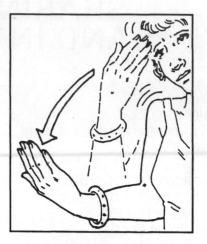
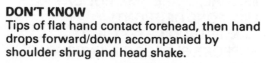

DON'T KNOW
Tips of flat hand contact forehead, then hand drops forward/down accompanied by shoulder shrug and head shake.

UNDERSTAND, REALISE, IDEA
Index finger flicks up at side of forehead. If located at the side of the eye, palm in, the meaning is AWARE, AWARENESS.

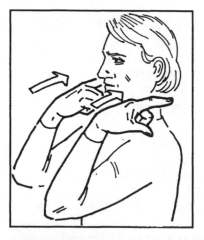

DON'T UNDERSTAND, OVER MY HEAD
Indexes flick simultaneously backwards at sides of head.

Sharing Ideas and Interests

BORED, BORING, TEDIOUS, DULL
Fingers of flat hand tap the chin twice.

EXCITED, INTEREST, INTERESTING
Tips of clawed hands contact chest and rub up and down alternately in quick movement. Also means: EAGER, KEEN. One hand may be used as a regional sign for TOILET.

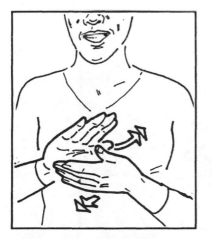

ENJOY, HAPPY, PLEASURE
Flat hands R. on top of L. brush against each other in repeated movement.

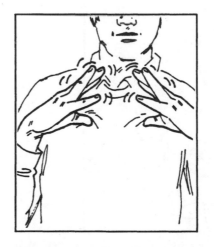

LEISURE, SPARE TIME, HOLIDAY
Thumb tips of open hands contact chest as fingers wiggle. One hand may be used.

Sharing Ideas and Interests

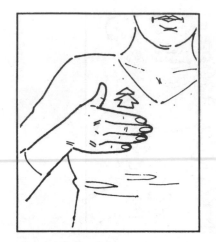

LIKE, FOND OF
Palm of flat hand taps chest twice. Also means: FRONT.

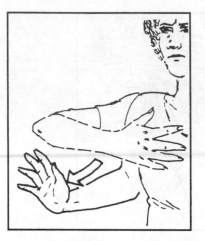

CAN'T STAND, DETEST, HATE
Open hand on upper chest twists to palm forward and pushes away from body with emphasis. **Face and body indicate negative form.**

SUPPORT, SUPPORTER
Closed hands with thumbs up move forward in small arc with stress. Movement is repeated for ENCOURAGE. **Variation:** Palm forward fists held in the air, wave from side to side or move up and down.

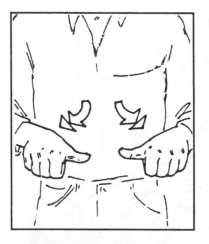

FAVOURITE, PREFERENCE
Palm down closed hands with thumbs extended make small repeated downward movements. Can be made with a single movement. May start with thumbs making short upward movement on the body before moving down.

Sharing Ideas and Interests

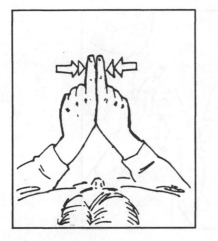

SAME, SIMILAR
Indexes pointing forward tap together twice.
Can be a single movement. Also means:
ALSO, TOO. If hands move apart with fingers
springing sharply open, the meaning is LIKE.

DIFFERENT, DIFFERENCE
Indexes together, pointing forward palms
down, move apart, twisting to palms up.

EASY, SIMPLE
The index finger prods the cheek twice. The
cheeks may be puffed out to mean DEAD
EASY, DODDLE. Also means: SOFT.

HARD, DIFFICULT, PROBLEM
R. thumb tip prods L. palm twice. **Variation:**
knuckles of R. fist move sharply down,
brushing against L. palm, to mean HARD,
FIRM.

Sharing Ideas and Interests

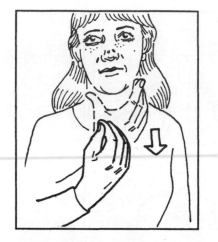

WISH, DESIRE, FANCY
Tips of fingers and thumb contact the throat; the hand moves forward as the fingers close onto the thumb. Also means: DRY, THIRSTY.

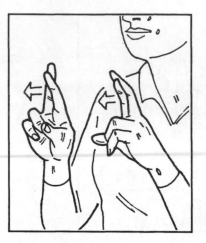

HOPE
Hands held pointing up, palm forward with index and middle fingers crossed. One hand may be used. With thumb extended, sign becomes NATIONAL LOTTERY. **Variation:** palm left R. full 'C' hand closes sharply to a fist in front of the mouth (regional).

WIN, SUCCEED, ACHIEVE
Palm left R. clawed hand moves sharply to the left, closing to a fist as it brushes across L. palm. **Variations:** 1. Closed hand makes small circular movements at head height. 2. Thumb tip brushes sharply down side of chest twisting to palm down (regional).

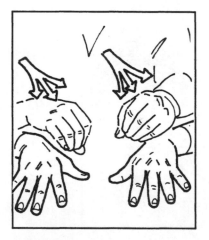

LOSE, DROP
Palm down full 'O' hands spring open, moving down and apart. If the sign is made palm up, the meaning is WASTE.

Sharing Ideas and Interests

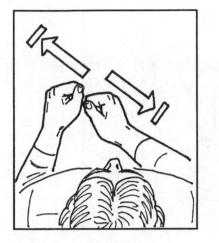

SPORT, ATHLETICS
Closed hands held together pull sharply diagonally apart twisting L. to palm down, R. to palm up.

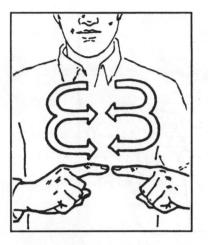

COMPETITION, FIXTURES
Indexes point in and make small movements towards each other as the hands move down.

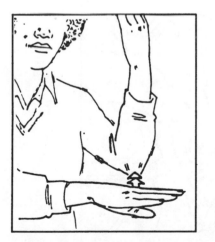

BOTTOM
Palm down R. flat hand taps left elbow twice (regional). **Variation**: palm down hand makes small repeated downward movement.

TOP, IMPORTANT
Palm down R. flat hand moves up in arc to contact palm onto tip of extended L. index finger. Contact may be repeated. Can start with R. full 'O' hand springing open to contact palm onto L. index.

Sharing Ideas and Interests

CANCEL, CALL OFF
R. index makes a cross on the L. palm.

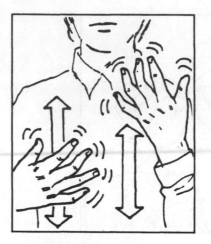

SCORE, RESULTS
Two palm back open hands move alternately
up and down in front of the body with
fingers wiggling. Also means MATHS.

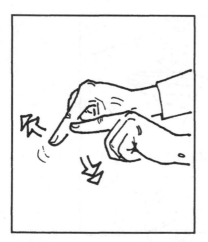

FOOTBALL
Indexes extended and pointing down; R.
flicks forward and L. back in sharp
movement. 'V' hands are sometimes used.
Variation: Fingers of palm back open hands
pointing in make short quick movements
towards each other (regional).

CRICKET
Closed hands move forward simultaneously
in batting action.

Sharing Ideas and Interests

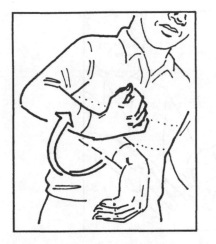

RUGBY
Cupped hand sweeps back and up to finish with backs of fingers in contact with side of body.

SWIM, BREAST-STROKE
Palm down flat hands move apart and backwards in action of swimming breast-stroke. May be signed with alternate overarm action of swimming as in CRAWL.

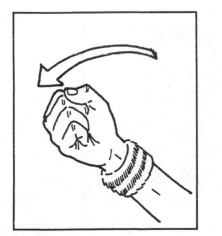

TENNIS
R. fist makes forward striking movement. May be preceded by L. 'O' hand moving up and springing open.

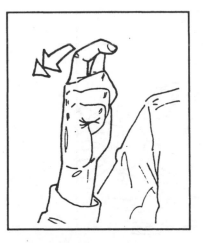

BADMINTON
R. closed hand with thumb tucked into bent index; hand makes short repeated bending movement from the wrist.

Sharing Ideas and Interests

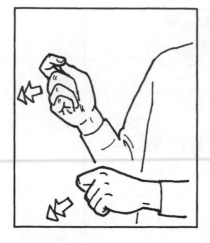

ANGLING, FISHING
Two closed hands with thumbs tucked into bent indexes, R. above L.; hands make short repeated bending movements from the wrists.

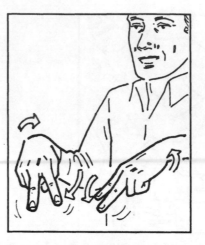

DANCE, DANCING
'V' hands make downward flicking movements from the wrists as hands move from left to right. 'N' hands may alternatively be used.

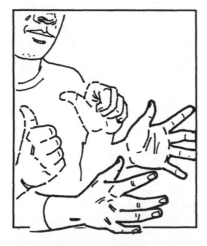

RETIRE, RETIREMENT
Thumb tips of palm facing closed hands contact upper chest, then hands move forward and spring open.

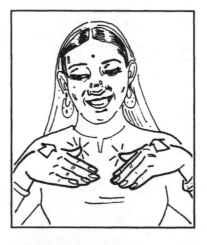

BREAK, REST, RELAX
Palm down flat hands make short movement back to contact upper chest.

Sharing Ideas and Interests

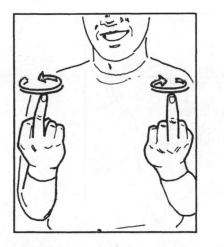

HOLIDAY
Extended middle fingers make small circular movements. One hand may be used.
Variations: 1. Flat hands at sides of head move forward/down twisting to palm down, twice. 2. Fingers of 'V' hands flexed against thumbs spring open as hands make small repeated forward movement. (All regional.)

CAMP, CAMPING, TENT
Two 'N' hands, held at an angle with fingertips touching, move apart/down. Flat hands may be used.

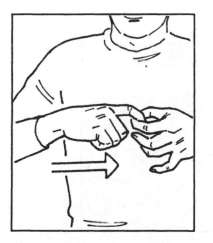

CARAVAN
R. index is hooked into L. 'O' hand; formation moves to left. **Variation:** tips of palm down 'Y' hands contact, then pull apart and slightly down.

HOTEL
Flat hands at sides of head move forward/down, twisting to palm down. One hand may be used. Short repeated movement can be used for regional sign for HOLIDAY. Also means: RESIDENTIAL, STAY OVER.

Sharing Ideas and Interests

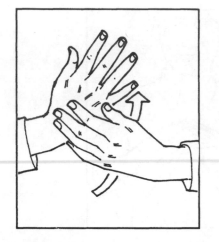

SPRING
R. open hand swivels to point upwards from behind L. If R. hand opens from full 'O' hand, the meaning is GROW, DEVELOP.

SUMMER
Index edge of bent hand contacts chin, then moves up in small forward arc to contact forehead. **Variation**: index edge of flat hand is drawn across the forehead, then shaken forward/down. As illustrated, also means: STRANGER (regional).

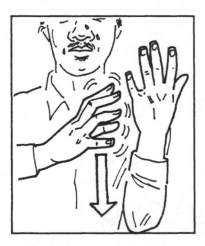

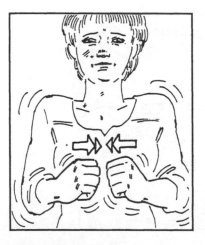

AUTUMN
R hand moves down with fingers fluttering from L. open hand. **Variation**: two 'N' hands move down, making alternate twisting movements.

WINTER, COLD
Closed hands make quick quivering movement, as elbows are drawn into the body with shoulders hunched.

Sharing Ideas and Interests

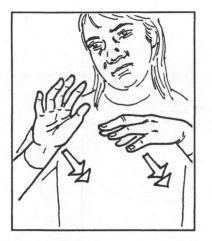

RAIN, RAINING
Palm down open hands move down simultaneously several times. If cheeks are puffed and movement exaggerated, the meaning is HEAVY RAIN, DOWNPOUR. If fingers flutter in soft downward movement, the meaning is SNOW, SNOWFALL.

SUN, SUNNY, SUNSHINE
Full 'O' hand held at head height moves in/down as hand opens. The hand can be located appropriate to context. Also means: LIGHT, LIGHT ON. For LIGHT OFF, hand starts open, then closes.

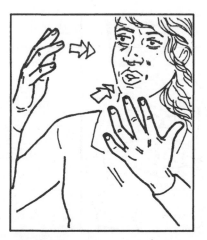

WIND, WINDY
Palm back open hands make repeated backward movement at head height. Hands may be palm in with side to side movement. One hand may be used.

WHICH? EITHER
Thumb and little finger extended, hand moves from side to side, or between the people or items being referred to. **Face and body indicate if question form**. Also means: BETWEEN.

Sharing Ideas and Interests

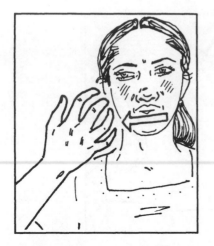

HOT, HEAT
R. palm back clawed hand moves sharply across the mouth from left to right. If a small circular movement is used, the meaning is WARM. **Variation**: index edge of palm down flat hand moves left to right across the forehead and shakes downwards.

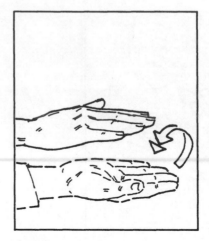

GARDEN
Flat hands turns over from palm up to palm down in repeated movement.

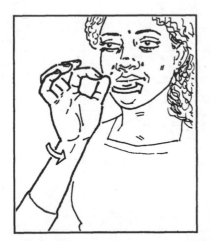

FLOWER
'O' hand moves from side to side in repeated movement under the nose. A bunched hand may alternatively be used.

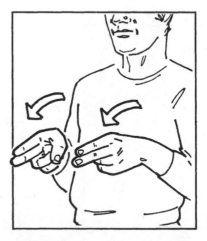

DEAD, DIE
Palm facing 'N' hands twist down sharply at the wrists to point forward. If the movement is slow, the sign produced is DYING.

Sharing Ideas and Interests

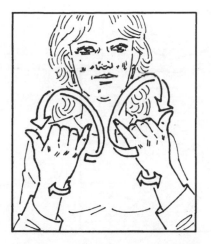

CELEBRATE, PARTY, HAVE FUN, SOCIAL
Thumbs and little fingers extended; hands move up/outwards in circles and rotate at the wrists. The cheeks may be puffed.

EASTER, EASTER EGG
Tips of clawed hands tap together twice (regional). **Variation:** tip of R. index finger draws a cross on the back of the L. hand.

BIRTHDAY
Blades of flat hands on sides of waist move forward/in then up and apart (regional). **Variation:** closed hand with thumb tucked into bent index makes repeated tugging movement at side of head (regional).

CHRISTMAS
Tips of R. flat hand brush backwards against back of L. hand, then R. hand closes and moves down to contact back of L. **Variation:** fingers and thumb hold and stroke down the chin, as fingers close onto the thumb.

Sharing Ideas and Interests

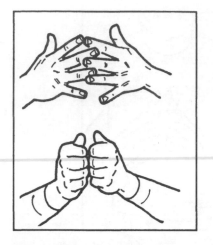

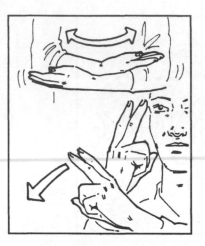

WEEKEND
Open hands come together in brief fingerspelt form of 'W', then pull slightly apart, change to closed hands and contact again. **Variation:** R. extended index moves down left forearm, changes to flat hand moving down to contact extended L. little finger.

BABYSIT, SITTER
Sign for 'baby', then two 'V' hands R. on top of L. move forward/down from near eye. If first part of sign is 'child', the meaning is CHILDCARE, CHILDMINDER.

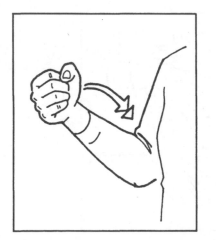

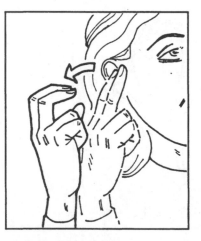

PUB, BAR
Palm left R. fist pulls backwards/down twice. L. hand is also sometimes included, palm down, below R. hand. **Variation:** R. cupped hand, palm left makes small repeated circular movements back towards the mouth.

DEAF CLUB
Tips of 'N' hand contact ear, then fingers bend into 'C' shape as hand moves slightly out (regional). Second part of sign may be signed with R. fist on top of L. or CLUB may be a fingerspelt pattern.

Sharing Ideas and Interests

CHURCH, CHAPEL
Two fists, R. on top of L.; formation makes repeated movement up and down.

CAR
Closed hands, palms in/up, move in action of steering wheel. If hands move simultaneously forwards, the meaning is DRIVE.

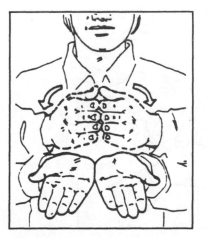

BOOK, CATALOGUE
Flat hands palm to palm twist open to palms up.

COMPUTER
'C' hands move in small simultaneous circles. **Variation:** fingers of palm down open hands move slightly from side to side as fingers wiggle to indicate COMPUTER KEYBOARD.

Sharing Ideas and Interests

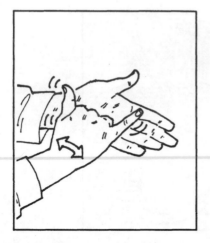

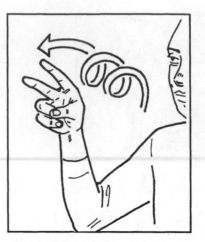

SHOP
R. hand with little finger and thumb extended makes small quick side to side movement on L. palm (regional). Also means: NEW YORK.

LOOK AROUND, SIGHTSEEING, TOUR
'V' hand pointing forward moves forward from near eye, twisting in repeated small circular movements from the wrist as the hand moves round in an arc. The first part of the sign on its own means LOOK (directional).

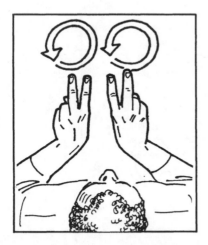

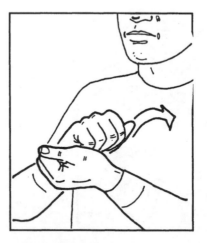

VIDEO
Palm down 'V' hands move in small horizontal circles simultaneously.

HIRE, BORROW
Closed hands, palms facing and crossed at the wrists move back/left to body in small arc. If the movement is forward and away from the signer, the sign becomes LEND.

Sharing Ideas and Interests

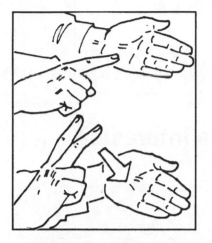

TV, TELEVISION, TELLY
Fingerspell 'T' 'V'. Sometimes index fingers are used, pointing forward and moving apart and down to trace outline of television. This version also means MONITOR, SCREEN.

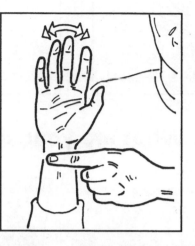

CINEMA, TV PROGRAMME
Heel of R. open hand contacts L. index and makes small side to side shaking movements. Formation may move down throughout.

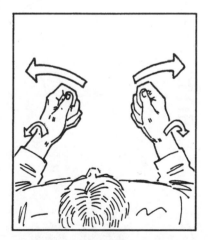

COMIC, MAGAZINE
Closed hands with thumbs tucked into bent indexes; hands twist at wrists from palm in to palm up in repeated movement. If hands start in contact and move up/apart, the sign produced is NEWSPAPER.

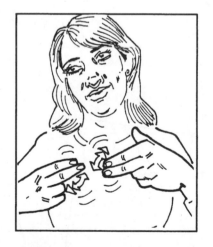

NEWS
Fingertips of 'N' hands brush against each other in repeated alternate forward and backward movement.

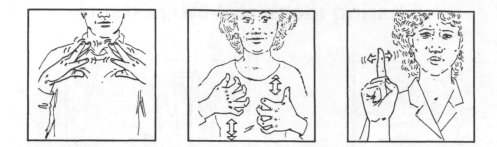

What are your spare time interests?

FOOTBALL

SWIMMING

COMPUTER

DANCING

DEAF CLUB

SPORT

TV

CINEMA

SHARING FEELINGS AND RELATIONSHIPS

FEEL, SENSE, EMOTION

CONFIDENCE, CONFIDENT (GAIN CONFIDENCE, LOSE CONFIDENCE)

NERVOUS, ANXIOUS, SCARED

DEPRESSED, SAD, DOWN IN THE DUMPS (RELIEF)

ENVIOUS, JEALOUS

LONELY, ISOLATED

GLAD, PLEASED, HAPPY (GREAT PLEASURE, DELIGHT)

HAD ENOUGH, FED UP (FULL)

BUSY, OVERWORKED

LAZY, IDLE

DISAPPOINTED, GUTTED (MISS)

TIRED, EXHAUSTED

PROUD (BOAST, SHOW OFF)

ANGRY, MAD, TEMPER

CRITICISE

PRAISE, CONGRATULATE (POPULAR)

BELIEVE, DON'T BELIEVE

HOW?

FORGET

REMEMBER (CONCEPT, GUESS)

ASK

DEMAND, CLAIM (COMMITTED TO, DEVOTED)

KEEP OUT OF, DON'T INTERFERE, BUTT OUT

PRIVATE, SECRET

NEED, WANT, WISH

BOND, LIAISON, RELATIONSHIP (UNITE, COORDINATE, ASSOCIATION)

LOVELY, TASTY (SWEET, PRETTY)

NICE, SWEET, DELICIOUS

START, BEGIN, COMMENCE

FINISH, COMPLETE (STOP)

FIRST

LAST

SINGLE, NOT MARRIED

DIVORCED (SPLIT UP, SEPARATED)

ENGAGED, FIANCE/E

MARRIED, WEDDING

NEW (MODERN)

MEET, FACE TO FACE

CONVERSE, DISCUSS, CORRESPOND (EXCHANGE, SWAP)

GO OUT WITH, PARTNER

VISIT

STAY, REMAIN, BE STILL (CARRY ON, CONTINUE, PERMANENT)

CONTACT, IN TOUCH, JOIN, LINK (LOSE CONTACT, DISCONNECT)

MINICOM, TEXT 'PHONE

ALLOW, PERMIT

BAN, DISALLOW, FORBID, TABOO

FIGHT (CLASH)

ARGUE, QUARREL

WILL, WOULD

WON'T, WOULDN'T

KISS (KISSING)

BYE, FAREWELL, CHEERIO

Sharing Feelings and Relationships

FEEL, SENSE, EMOTION
Tips of middle fingers contact body in upward brushing movement. One hand may be used. Movement may be repeated. Open hands may be used.

CONFIDENCE, CONFIDENT
Index edge of R. 'C' hand taps twice against chest. If the sign makes a short upward movement the meaning is GAIN CONFIDENCE. If the hand makes a short downward movement the meaning is LOSE CONFIDENCE.

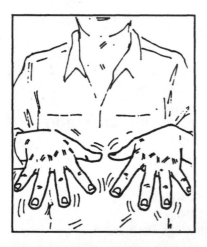

NERVOUS, ANXIOUS, SCARED
Hands held loose pointing down (can be indexes only) shake repeatedly from the wrists. **Variations:** 1. Edge of R. index pointing left held over heart makes quick up and down movement. 2. R. 'R' hand palm back taps chest over heart several times in quick movement.

DEPRESSED, SAD, DOWN IN THE DUMPS
Index edge of palm down flat hands brushes down body. **Face and body indicate appropriate emotion** and can change the meaning to RELIEF.

Sharing Feelings and Relationships

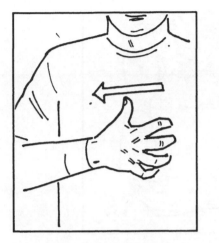

ENVIOUS, JEALOUS
Tips of R. clawed hand are drawn left to right across chest. **Variation:** bent index finger held between the teeth.

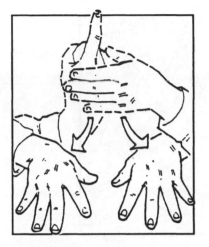

LONELY, ISOLATED
R. index extended and pointing up moves down behind L. hand then both hands open and swing to point down.

GLAD, PLEASED, HAPPY
Flat hand rubs in circular movement on the chest. **Variation:** tips of R. 'V' hand stand on L. palm and jump up and down with flexing movement meaning GREAT PLEASURE, DELIGHT. **Face and body indicate appropriate emotion.**

HAD ENOUGH, FED UP
Backs of fingers of bent hand are brought up sharply to contact underside of the chin. Movement may be repeated. **Face and body indicate appropriate emotion** and can change the meaning to FULL.

Sharing Feelings and Relationships

BUSY, OVERWORKED
Blade of R. flat hand swivels forward/down over index edge of L. hand. Movement may be repeated. Cheeks may be puffed.

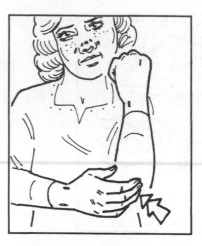

LAZY, IDLE
The palm of R. hand taps left elbow twice.
Variation: middle fingers extended and pointing up; hands make small repeated downward movement.

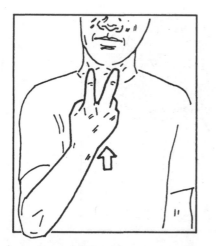

DISAPPOINTED, GUTTED
Tips of 'V' hands pointing up/back, jab into throat. The lips are pressed together. This is also a regional sign meaning MISS.

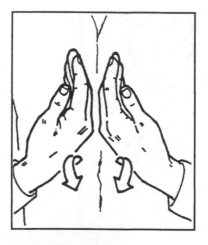

TIRED, EXHAUSTED
Tips of palm back bent hands contact upper chest, then hands twist and flop down so that blades contact chest. One hand may be used.

Sharing Feelings and Relationships

PROUD
Extended thumbs brush down chest in
alternate repeated backward circles. **Face
and body indicate appropriate emotion** and
can change meaning to BOAST, SHOW OFF.

ANGRY, MAD, TEMPER
Clawed hands with thumbs held straight
make sharp movement up and apart on
body, finishing palm up. Alternate upward
clawing movement is sometimes used. **Face
and body indicate appropriate emotion.**

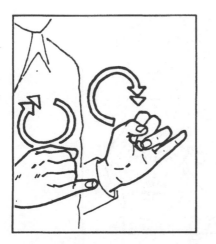

CRITICISE
Hands held palms facing, with little fingers
extended, move in alternate circles in the
direction appropriate to the context, e.g.
forwards in 'criticising you', or backwards in
'criticising me' and so on.

PRAISE, CONGRATULATE
Closed hands, with thumbs extended and
palms facing, move in alternate circles in the
direction appropriate to the context. A
smaller and quicker movement is used for
POPULAR.

Sharing Feelings and Relationships

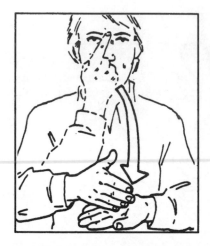

BELIEVE
Tip of R. index contacts forehead; hand moves down changing to flat hand, blade down on L. palm. For DON'T BELIEVE, sign ends with R. hand brushing sharply along and away from L. hand, accompanied by head shake.

HOW?
Clawed hands with thumbs extended tap backs of knuckles together twice. Can be palm up or palm back. **Face and body indicate question form.**

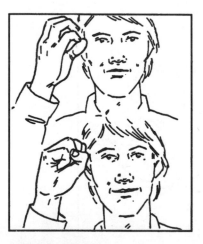

FORGET
Tips of R. full 'O' hand contact forehead, then hand springs open and forward.

REMEMBER
R. clawed hand closes sharply to fist at side of forehead. (R. fist can move down, palm down, to contact palm up L. fist at end of sign.) If the R. clawed hand moves across forehead closing to fist, the meaning is CONCEPT, GUESS.

Sharing Feelings and Relationships

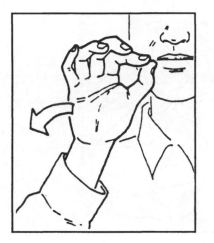

ASK
R. 'O' hand palm left moves forward from side of mouth in small arc, for contexts such as 'I'll ask', or is held forward and moves back to signer for contexts such as 'ask me', and so on.

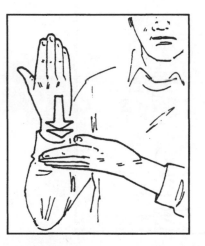

DEMAND, CLAIM
Back of palm up R. flat hand contacts L. palm twice with emphasis. A single movement can be used. Sometimes the R. hand only is used. If the sign begins with R. index contacting forehead, the meaning is COMMITTED TO, DEVOTED.

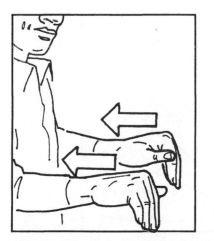

KEEP OUT OF, DON'T INTERFERE, BUTT OUT
Palm down bent hands pull back towards body. Head and shoulders move back slightly and lips are pressed together.

PRIVATE, SECRET
Index edge of flat hand taps mouth twice.
Variation: flat hands pointing up, R. in front of L., make slight alternate side to side movements in front of mouth.

Sharing Feelings and Relationships

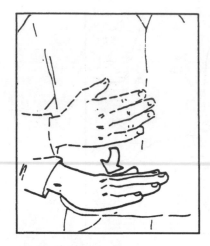

NEED, WANT, WISH
Flat hand brushes down side of body, twisting to palm down.

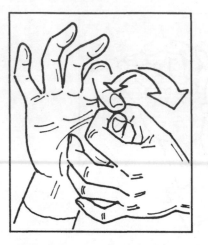

BOND, LIAISON, RELATIONSHIP
Interlinked 'O' hands make repeated backward and forward movement. The formation can be moved in horizontal circle, to mean UNITE, COORDINATE, ASSOCIATION.

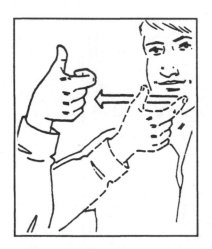

LOVELY, TASTY
R. index and thumb extended; index moves across chin left to right and closes, leaving thumb extended. Sign may start with index contacting the upper cheek, meaning SWEET, PRETTY.

NICE, SWEET, DELICIOUS
R. thumb tip moves across chin from left to right.

Sharing Feelings and Relationships

START, BEGIN, COMMENCE
R. hand with thumb up brushes down sharply behind L. flat hand. **Variation:** open hands pointing down bend sharply upwards to palm forward and snap shut.

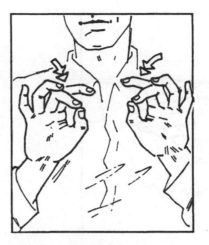

FINISH, COMPLETE
Middle fingers close onto ball of thumbs several times, quickly (regional). One hand may be used. **Variations:** 1. Closed hands with thumbs up move outwards in circles. 2. Open hands snap shut onto thumbs. This version also means STOP.

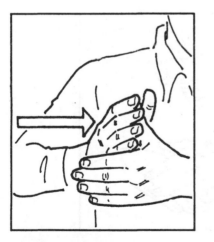

FIRST
Fingers of R. flat hand strike inside of L. thumb. **Variation:** palm forward index twists sharply to palm back with slight upward movement.

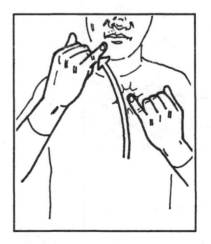

LAST
Tip of R. little finger strikes tip of L. little finger in sharp upward movement (or can be downward movement). **Variation:** R. flat hand moves down so edge touches L. little finger.

Sharing Feelings and Relationships

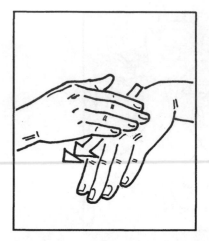

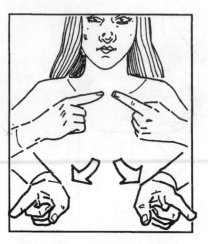

SINGLE, NOT MARRIED
R. flat hand brushes forward twice along back of palm down L. hand (regional).
Variation: R. index extended, palm back moves down/forward behind L. flat hand.

DIVORCED
Index tips contact each other, then hands swing apart to point forward. 'N' hands are sometimes used. **Variation**: palm down bent hands, pointing in, move apart. This version also means SPLIT UP, SEPARATED.

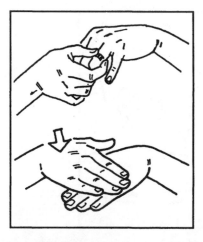

ENGAGED, FIANCE/E
Tip of extended R. index finger, slightly bent, flips over from palm up to palm down, contacting back of L. ring finger. A straight R. index finger is also sometimes used.

MARRIED, WEDDING
R. index and thumb move along L. ring finger (R. middle finger and thumb can also be used), then R. flat hand moves down onto back of L. hand.

Sharing Feelings and Relationships

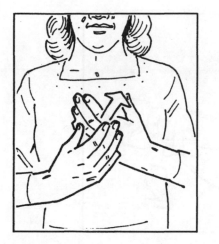

NEW
R. flat hand brushes up back of L. Repeated movement may be used to mean MODERN.

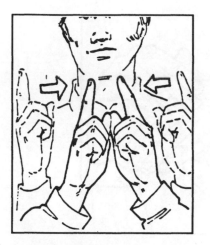

MEET, FACE TO FACE
Indexes held apart move in to meet each other. Direction of movement can be varied to suit context.

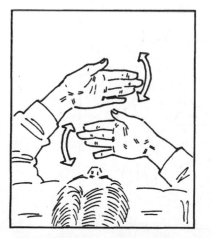

CONVERSE, DISCUSS, CORRESPOND
Palm up flat hands one above the other move to and fro across each other in front of the body. Direction of movement can be varied to suit context. If hands cross each other in a single movement the meaning is EXCHANGE, SWAP.

GO OUT WITH, PARTNER
L. index, middle finger and thumb hold fingers of R. 'N' hand; formation moves in small horizontal circle.

Sharing Feelings and Relationships

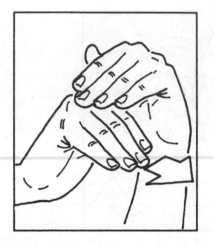

VISIT
R. bent hand faces and moves under L. bent hand in the direction appropriate to the context, e.g. forwards in 'I'll visit you', or backwards in 'come and visit' and so on (regional).

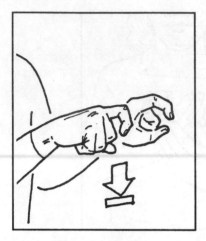

STAY, REMAIN, BE STILL
Palm down 'C' hands make short, firm movement down. One hand may be used. If hands move simultaneously forwards or sideways, the meaning is CARRY ON, CONTINUE, PERMANENT.

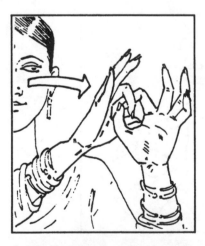

CONTACT, IN TOUCH, JOIN, LINK
Open hands move together and interlock index fingers and thumbs. Movement can be in the direction appropriate to the context. If the sign is reversed so that the interlocked fingers spring open and apart, the meaning is LOSE CONTACT, DISCONNECT.

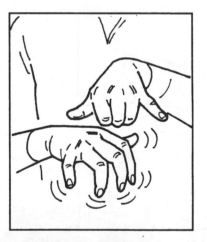

MINICOM, TEXT 'PHONE
Palm down L. closed hand with little finger and thumb extended, held forward/above R. open hand; R. hand fingers wiggle in slight side to side movement. Formation can move forwards in contexts such as 'I'll call you' or backwards as in 'call me'.

Sharing Feelings and Relationships

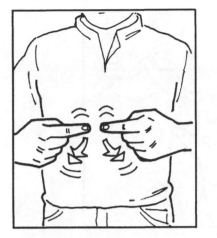

ALLOW, PERMIT
Indexes point towards each other, then swing down/apart in small repeated movement.

BAN, DISALLOW, FORBID, TABOO
Closed hands start crossed and pull sharply apart, twisting to palm down. Little fingers may be extended. Sometimes flat hands are used. **Face and body indicate negative form.**

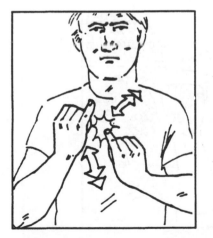

FIGHT
Little fingers bang together several times. If the little fingers are brought together in one movement the meaning is CLASH.

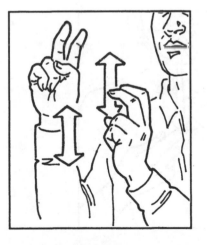

ARGUE, QUARREL
Index and middle fingers, extended and bent, held palms facing; hands move alternately up and down.

Sharing Feelings and Relationships

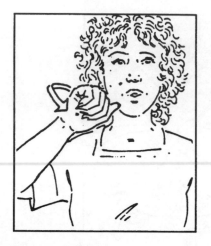

WILL, WOULD
Palm forward closed hand twists
forward/down at side of chin.

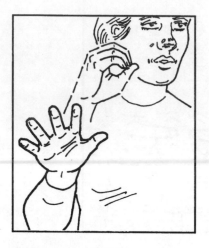

WON'T, WOULDN'T
Fingers flexed behind thumb; hand moves
sharply forward/down from side of chin and
springs open.

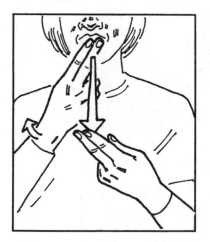

KISS
Tips of R. 'N' hand touch lips, then move
down to contact tips of L. 'N' hand. 'N' hands
can repeat contact, twisting R. on L., then L.
on R. to mean KISSING. **Variation:** tips of
bunched hands contact each other.

BYE, FAREWELL, CHEERIO
Flat hand flexes up and down. Movement
can be a small side to side wave.

How do you feel?

PLEASED

FED UP

LONELY

DISAPPOINTED

HAPPY

TIRED

CONFIDENT

SAD

FOOD AND DRINK

DRINK
WATER (THIRSTY)
WINE
LEMONADE, POP, FIZZY DRINK
TEA, CUPPA
COFFEE (COCA COLA)
SUGAR
MILK
EAT, FOOD
HUNGRY, STARVING, FAMISHED
BREAKFAST (MORNING)
DINNER, MEAL (SHEFFIELD)
MEAT (KILL)
CHICKEN (BIRD)
TURKEY
BEEF
SAUSAGES
BURGER
SPAGHETTI
CHIPS
POTATO
MASH
PEAS
CARROT
FISH AND CHIPS (WHITBY)
FISH CAKE
FISH FINGERS
KETCHUP, SAUCE
BREAD
BUTTER
BAKED BEANS
TOAST, GRILL

SALAD
TOMATO
LETTUCE
ONION (CRY, TEARS)
PIZZA
SANDWICH
CHEESE
EGG
FRUIT
ORANGE
APPLE
BANANA
STRAWBERRY
CHERRY
PEACH
PEAR
PLUM
PUDDING, DESSERT (SOUP, CEREAL)
JELLY
CUSTARD
CAKE
CREAM
CHOCOLATE (JEALOUS)
NUTS
BISCUIT
CRISPS
SWEETS
ICE-CREAM
PICNIC
PARTY
MORE
ENOUGH, PLENTY

Food and Drink

DRINK
Full 'C' hand moves upwards and tilts backwards near mouth. Movement may be repeated.

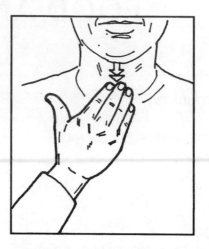

WATER
Flat hand changes to bent hand twice as tips brush downwards on the throat. This version also means THIRSTY. **Variations:** 1. Tips of palm back cupped hand brush upward on the cheek twice. 2. Thumb tip of 'Y' hand brushes forward twice on the cheek. (All regional.)

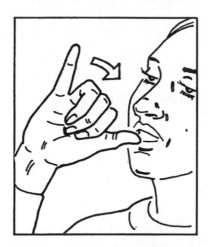

WINE
Palm left R. 'Y' hand tilts backwards near the mouth.

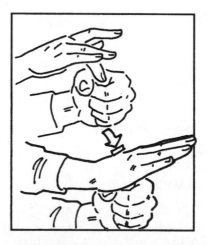

LEMONADE, POP, FIZZY DRINK
R. middle finger brushes against top of L. fist, then changes to open hand, brought sharply down onto L. fist. This sign is also sometimes used as a term of abuse, with appropriate expression of emotion.

Food and Drink

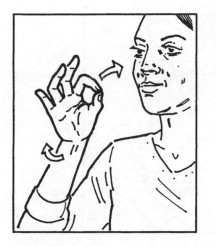

TEA, CUPPA
Palm left R. 'O' hand tips backwards near mouth.

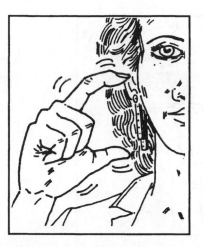

COFFEE
Palm left R. 'C' hand makes several small quick twisting movements near mouth. If the hand makes two short forward movements from side to side, the meaning is COCA COLA. **Variation**: edge of R. fist on top of L. rubs in small circular movements.

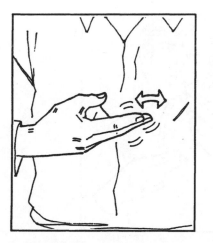

SUGAR
Palm up 'N' hand makes small side to side shaking movements.

MILK
Closed hands make short alternate movements up and down. Sometimes a slight squeezing action is used. Hands may rub against each other.

109

Food and Drink

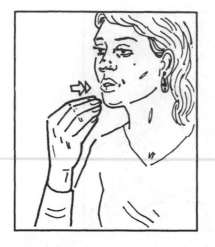

EAT, FOOD
Bunched hand makes small repeated
movement backwards towards the mouth.

HUNGRY, STARVING, FAMISHED
Tips of bent hands held against lower chest;
the hands flop down from the wrists with the
fingertips maintaining contact with the body.

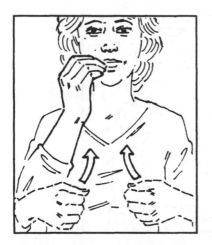

BREAKFAST
Closed hands move up the body from the
waist, then bunched hand makes two small
movements backwards towards the mouth.
The first part of this sign is a regional sign
for MORNING. The second part of the sign
only can be used.

DINNER, MEAL
Two palm back 'N' hands move alternately
up to the mouth. **Variation:** edge of R. 'N'
hand moves in small sawing action against
edge of L. 'N' hand. This version also means
SHEFFIELD.

Food and Drink

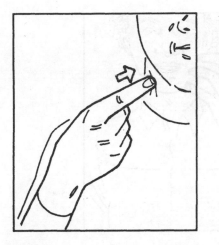

MEAT
Tip of R. index finger prods into the side of the neck. Movement may be repeated.
Variation: cheek is grasped between thumb and bent index. As illustrated, also means KILL.

CHICKEN
Index and thumb pointing forward open and close near mouth, as elbow makes small movement in and out from side of body. If the sign is made without the movement of the elbow, the meaning is BIRD.

TURKEY
Index, middle finger and thumb extended and pointing down; back of hand contacts the chin and hand makes small shaking movement.

BEEF
Tip of extended thumb prods into the side of the neck (regional).

Food and Drink

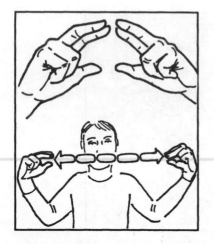

SAUSAGES
Finger of 'N' hands close onto thumbs repeatedly as hands move apart.

BURGER
Palm back full 'C' hand makes small repeated backward movement towards the mouth. Two hands can be used, held together. **Variation:** two clawed hands, R. on top of L., reverse to L. on top of R.

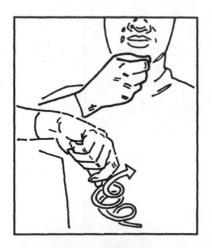

SPAGHETTI
Thumb tucked into bent index; hand moves in twisting movement from the wrist, then moves up towards the mouth.

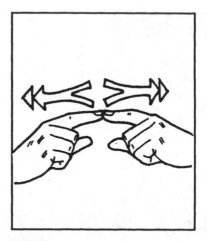

CHIPS
Tip of R. index and thumb contact tip of L. index and thumb; hands move slightly apart several times as fingertips close onto thumbs in quick repeated movement.

Food and Drink

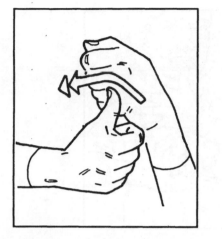

POTATO
Edge of R. thumb brushes against L. closed hand in repeated movement.

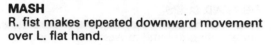

MASH
R. fist makes repeated downward movement over L. flat hand.

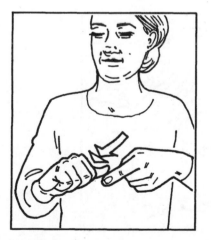

PEAS
R. thumb scrapes forward several times along L. index (regional).

CARROT
Palm forward R. fist held near mouth twists sharply to palm back.

Food and Drink

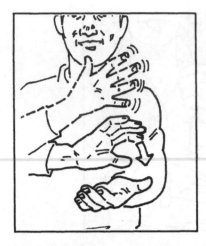

FISH AND CHIPS
Thumb of R. open hand contacts chin as
fingers wiggle; hand moves down changing
to full 'C' hand making repeated shaking
movement above L. palm up cupped hand.
The first part of this sign is a regional sign
for WHITBY.

FISH CAKE
Thumb of R. open hand contacts chin as
fingers wiggle, then moves down changing
to a clawed hand, contacting back of L. palm
down flat hand.

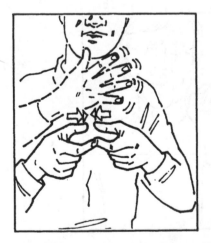

FISH FINGERS
Thumb of R. open hand contacts chin as
fingers wiggle, then tips of index fingers and
thumbs tap together twice.

KETCHUP, SAUCE
R. flat hand bangs repeatedly against edge
of L. full 'C' hand. **Variation**: palm forward R.
full 'C' hand twists over in repeated shaking
movement.

Food and Drink

BREAD
Edge of R. flat hand makes small sawing movement on L. palm.

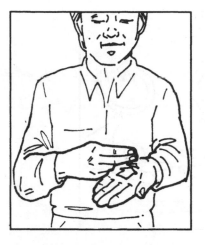

BUTTER
Edge of R. 'N' hand makes small repeated scraping movement on L. palm.

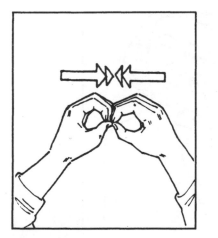

BAKED BEANS
Tips of fingerspelt 'B' formation tap together twice.

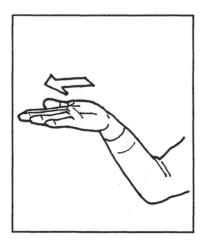

TOAST, GRILL
Palm up flat hand makes short movement forward. Two hands may be used.

115

Food and Drink

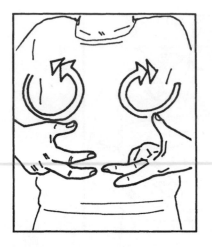

SALAD
Index, middle fingers and thumbs extended
and pointing in; hands move in
simultaneous repeated circular movements.

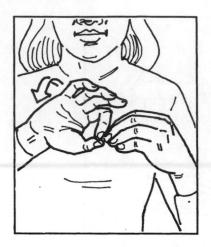

TOMATO
Tips of R. 'O' hand contact and twist away
from tips of L. bunched hand.

LETTUCE
Heels of slightly cupped hands tap together
twice (regional).

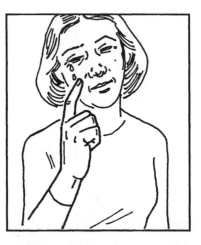

ONION
Index moves down the cheek with slight
twisting movement. Can be made with a
flexing movement of the index, or repeated
downward brushing movement. Also
means: CRY, TEARS.

116

Food and Drink

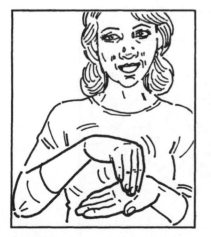

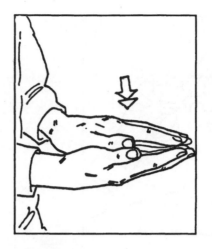

PIZZA
R. index pointing down moves in large circle above L. palm up flat hand.

SANDWICH
Palm together flat hands tap together twice.
Variation: two bunched hands, held together, palm back, held near mouth.

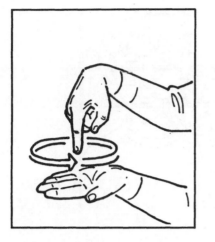

CHEESE
Tips of R. bent hand contact L. palm; R. hand rocks slightly from side to side, or backwards and forwards, as tips maintain contact.

EGG
Palm up R. 'N' hand makes slicing movement above L. fist. Sometimes, R. bent index is used. **Variation**: tips of bent 'V' hands contact each other as hands twist down/apart.

Food and Drink

FRUIT
Palm back hand with index, middle finger and thumb extended and bent makes small upward circular movement in front of mouth. Movement can be repeated.

ORANGE
Palm left R. full 'C' hand closes to a fist several times at side of mouth. Sometimes a clawed hand is used with fingers flexing.

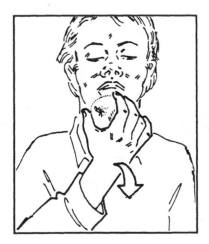

APPLE
Palm back full 'C' hand twists to palm up in small upward movement in front of mouth. Movement can be repeated. Sometimes a clawed hand is used.

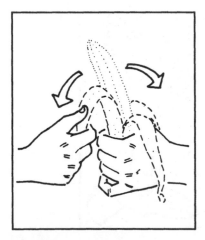

BANANA
R. index finger and thumb contact each other in repeated downward movement above L. fist in action of peeling a banana. **Variation:** tips of index fingers and thumbs contact each other, then hands move apart in small arc as fingers close onto thumbs in shape of banana.

Food and Drink

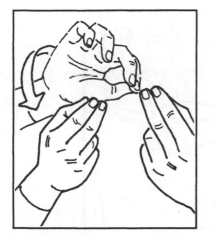

STRAWBERRY
Tips of index, middle fingers and thumbs
contact each other, then R. hand moves and
twists away from L. hand.

CHERRY
R. 'V' hand pointing down and palm back
makes small side to side shaking movement
at side of head.

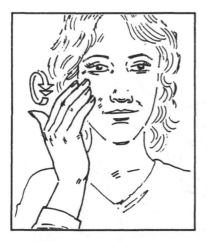

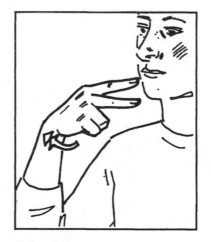

PEACH
Fingertips make small circular rubbing
movement on the cheek.

PEAR
Tips of R. 'V' hand make small forward
brushing movement near side of the mouth.
Variation: tips of palm forward 'N' hand
touch side of mouth and twist to palm back.

Food and Drink

PLUM
R. bunched hand holds end of L. thumb, then moves and twists away from L. hand.

PUDDING, DESSERT
Palm down R. hand with thumb tucked into bent index twists to palm back in repeated upward movement near the mouth. Sometimes made with palm up R. 'N' hand. Also means: SOUP, CEREAL.

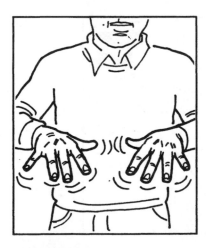

JELLY
Palm down open hands make short repeated shaking movements. Sign can be made with a palm down clawed hand.

CUSTARD
Thumb and little finger extended, tilted to thumb down; hand moves in horizontal circular movement (regional).

Food and Drink

CAKE
Tips of R. clawed hand contact back of L. hand. Contact may be repeated.

CREAM
Tip of little finger strokes across bottom lip.

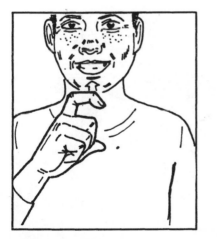

CHOCOLATE
Index edge of R. 'C' hand taps against the chin twice (regional). Also means: JEALOUS.

NUTS
Heel of hand with fingers bent at second knuckles taps side of chin twice.

Food and Drink

BISCUIT
Tips of R. clawed hand tap twice near left elbow.

CRISPS
Tips of R. bunched hand contact L. palm, then hand twists and moves upwards towards the mouth. An 'O' hand is sometimes used. Movement may be repeated.

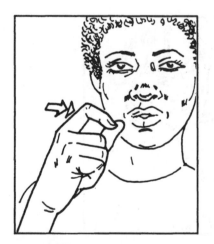

SWEETS
Tips of thumb and index finger contact each other and tap against the side of the mouth in repeated movement (regional).

ICE-CREAM
R. fist makes two small movements downwards in front of the mouth.

Food and Drink

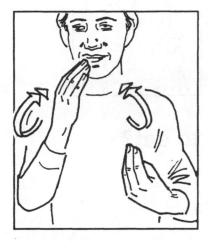

PICNIC
Bunched hands make alternate repeated movements upwards, towards the mouth.

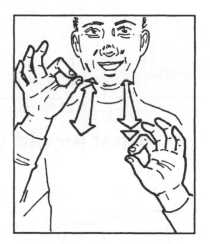

PARTY
'O' hands move up and down alternately, towards the mouth (regional). **Variation:** two 'Y' hands held near sides of head twist at wrists and move in circular movements.

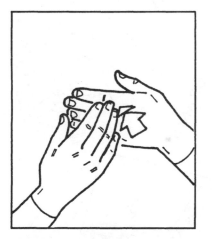

MORE
Palm back R. hand taps against back of L. hand twice. **Variation:** palm back R. hand contacts back of L. hand, then moves forward.

ENOUGH, PLENTY
Backs of the fingers of R. bent hand, palm back, brush upwards/forwards under the chin twice.

What would you like to eat?

APPLE CRISPS SANDWICH

FISH AND CHIPS BANANA SALAD

SPAGHETTI ORANGE

COLOUR AND TIME AND THIS AND THAT

DISABILITY, DISABLED

LAW, RULE (DECIDE, RULES, POLICY)

SHOULD, OUGHT (MUST)

MAKE, CREATE

CAN'T, COULDN'T, IMPOSSIBLE

DON'T, NOT, NOT ALLOWED

HAVEN'T, HAVEN'T GOT

NOTHING, NONE

AGREE, SUIT, SUITABLE (APPOINTMENT, BOOKING, DISAGREE)

REMIND (ASK, TELL)

TOILET

HOSPITAL

CLEAN

DIRTY

WET, DAMP, MOIST

DRY (SOLVE, DISSOLVE, CREMATE)

COLOUR

BLUE (ASIAN, ETHNIC MINORITY)

BLACK (BLACK PERSON, WHITE PERSON)

BROWN

PURPLE

RED

YELLOW (YEAR)

WHITE

GREEN

GREY

ORANGE

PINK

SILVER

GOLD

DARK/LIGHT (EVENING, NIGHT, DAY)

RAINBOW

MORNING, GOOD MORNING

AFTERNOON

NIGHT, EVENING

TIME, WHAT TIME?

WHEN?

EVERY DAY, DAILY

SOMETIMES (SHIFT WORK)

NEVER

ALWAYS, REGULAR, USUAL

ALL THE TIME

NOT YET

LATE (LATER, AFTER)

EARLY, EARLIER

HOUR, HOURLY

DAY

DATE (NUMBER, CALENDAR)

NOW (TODAY)

USE, USEFUL

LEARN, ABSORB, TAKE IN

THAT'S ALL!

Colour and Time and This and That

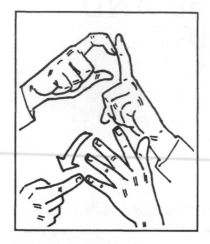

DISABILITY, DISABLED
Fingerspelt 'D' formation followed by R. index tip drawn down along fingers of L. hand.

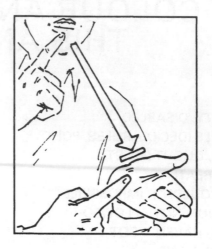

LAW, RULE
Index moves down from mouth to contact side down onto L. palm with emphasis. If the sign starts from the forehead the meaning is DECIDE. If the final movement is repeated down L. palm and wrist the meaning becomes RULES, POLICY.

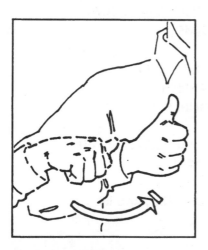

SHOULD, OUGHT
Palm down R. closed hand moves sharply down/in, twisting at the wrist to palm back with emphasis. Also means: MUST.

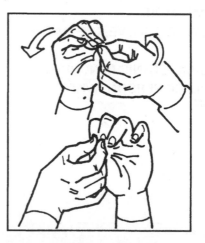

MAKE, CREATE
Bunched hands contact at fingertips, change position and contact again.

Colour and Time and This and That

CAN'T, COULDN'T, IMPOSSIBLE
Extended index, palm forward/down; hand moves down, looping over to finish palm up, accompanied by head shake. Both hands may be used. The sign may start with index contacting forehead. **Face and body indicate negative form**.

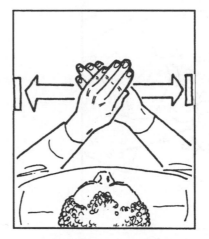

DON'T, NOT, NOT ALLOWED
Palm down flat hands start crossed, then swing sharply apart with emphasis, accompanied by head shake. **Face and body indicate negative form**.

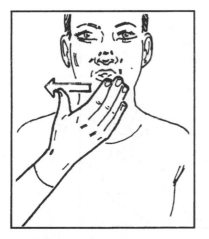

HAVEN'T, HAVEN'T GOT
Flat hand brushes sharply across the mouth left to right, as air is blown through the lips.

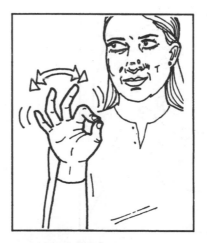

NOTHING, NONE
Palm forward 'O' hand shakes from side to side. Tip of the tongue protrudes between the teeth. Full 'O' hand can be used. Both hands can be used. The movement can be circular. **Face and body indicate negative form**.

Colour and Time and This and That

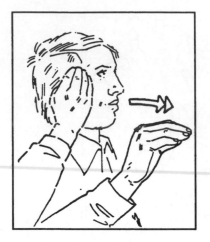

AGREE, SUIT, SUITABLE
Closed hands with thumbs up move in to contact each other. Contact may be repeated. Also means: APPOINTMENT, BOOKING (thumbs may not be prominent). If hands spring open and apart at the end of the sign accompanied by head shake, the meaning is DISAGREE.

REMIND
Bunched hand moves from temple in the direction of the person referred to with repeated final movement. Can twist and move back to contact shoulder as in 'remind me'. A bent hand can be used. The first part of the sign can be omitted for ASK, TELL.

TOILET
R. index tip taps edge of L. flat hand twice in fingerspelt 'T' formation. **Variations:** 1. Tip of extended index contacts forehead then chin. 2. Tips of clawed hand (can be middle finger only) contact chest in small up/down rubbing movement.

HOSPITAL
Tip of R. thumb draws a small cross on the left upper arm. The index fingertip can be used. **Variations:** 1. Palm back flat hands move in alternate forward circles round each other. 2. Flat hands pointing forward, palms facing, move simultaneously in small forward circles.

Colour and Time and This and That

CLEAN
Palm down R. flat hand brushes along the L. palm.

DIRTY
Open hands at right angles rub from side to side against each other palm to palm. Can also be made with circular movement. The nose may be wrinkled.

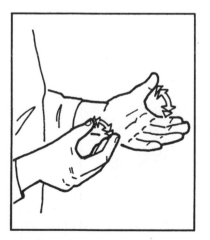

WET, DAMP, MOIST
Palm up bent hands open and close onto ball of thumbs twice. One hand may be used.

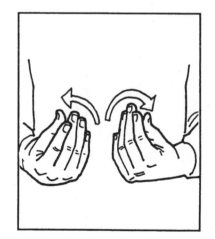

DRY
The thumb tips rub across the pads of the fingers. One hand may be used. If the hands move apart, the meaning is SOLVE, DISSOLVE. If the hands move forward, the meaning is CREMATE.

Colour and Time and This and That

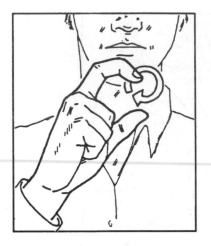

COLOUR
Palm left R. 'C' hand makes small vertical circles near side of chin. **Variations:** 1. Palm forward open hand makes small anticlockwise circles. 2. Middle fingertip of palm back open hand contacts chin, then hand moves and twists forwards while shaking (regional).

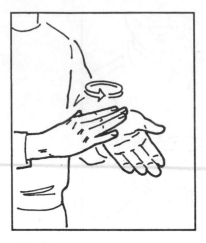

BLUE
R. flat hand makes small anticlockwise circle on L. palm or wrist. Can be made on back of palm down L. hand. If L. hand is palm back, the meaning is ASIAN, ETHNIC MINORITY.

BLACK
Closed hand moves forward/down along side of cheek. If a flat hand is used, the meaning is BLACK PERSON, WHITE PERSON.

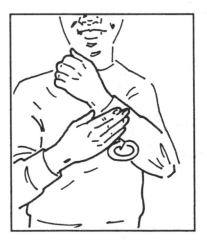

BROWN
R. flat hand makes small anticlockwise circle on the left forearm. **Variation:** tip of thumb and index finger rub together as hand moves forward from side of mouth (regional).

Colour and Time and This and That

PURPLE
Tips of R. 'O' hand brush forward twice off tip of L. index. **Variation:** fingertips of R. flat hand contact lips then make small anticlockwise circle on L. hand; can be palm, wrist or back of hand (regional).

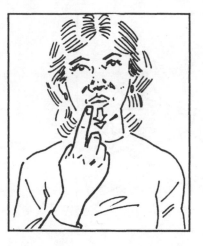

RED
Index brushes down bottom lip twice, bending slightly.

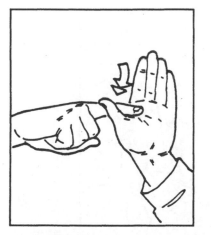

YELLOW
Hands in the fingerspelt 'Y' formation; index finger makes repeated downward brushing movement on base of L. thumb. If made with a single movement, also means YEAR. **Variation:** palm in clawed hand held at side of head makes several short, quick twisting movements (regional).

WHITE
Tips of 'O' hand make short repeated downward brushing movement near to the neck. The index fingertip can be used.

Colour and Time and This and That

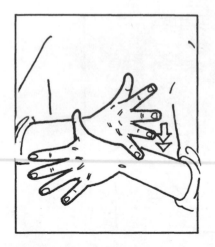

GREEN
Open hands crossed at the wrists tap together twice. **Variations**: 1. Palm down R. flat hand brushes up left arm. 2. Index edge of palm down R. flat hand taps twice on left upper chest. 3. Middle finger flicks against left shoulder. 4. Index finger brushes forward off nose. (All regional.)

GREY
Closed hands with little fingers extended, R. on top of L. at right angles; R. hand rubs against L. in small anticlockwise circles. Just closed hands can be used. **Variation:** index and thumb tip contact upper chest and move forward slightly, rubbing together.

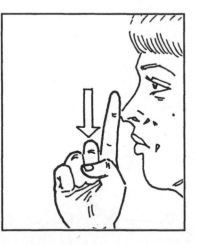

ORANGE
Clawed hand closes to a fist in repeated action at side of mouth.

PINK
R. index finger extended from a full 'O' hand, palm left, brushes down in contact with the nose. The little finger may also be extended. The movement can be a small brushing movement to the left.

Colour and Time and This and That

SILVER
R. little finger, slightly bent, rests on L. little finger, then both hands spring open and apart.

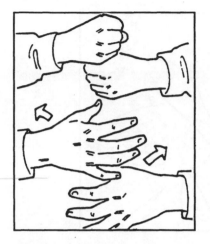

GOLD
Two fists contact each other, R. on top of L., then spring open and apart.

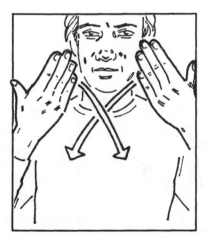

DARK/LIGHT
Two flat hands, palm back and pointing up, swing in/down to cross each other for DARK (also means EVENING, NIGHT). The sign is reversed, with the hands starting crossed and swinging up/apart for LIGHT (also means DAY).

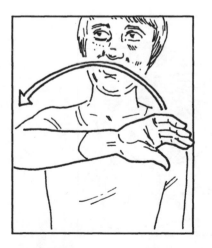

RAINBOW
Full 'C' hand palm forward and pointing left, held across the body, swings from the elbow up and to the right.

133

Colour and Time and This and That

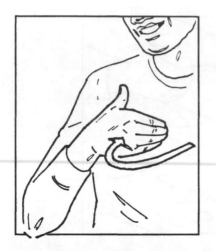

MORNING, GOOD MORNING
Fingertips of R. bent hand (with thumb up) contact left upper chest, then move in small arc and contact the right upper chest. Can be made with two bent hands moving up the chest, or two closed hands with thumbs up (regional).

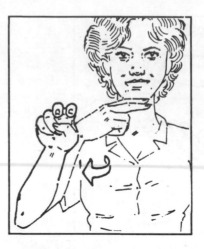

AFTERNOON
Tips of 'N' hand contact chin, then hand twists to point forward. **Variation**: two 'N' hands pointing in; R. twists to point forward, brushing against tips of L. (regional).

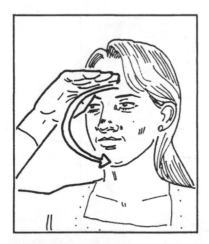

NIGHT, EVENING
Index edge of bent hand contacts forehead, then chin (regional). **Variations**: 1. Palm back flat hands pointing up swing in/down to cross each other. 2. Palm back bent 'V' hand makes two small backward movements in front of nose (regional).

TIME, WHAT TIME?
R. index tip taps the back of L. wrist several times. **Variation**: edge of R. upright index makes small repeated forward movement on L. palm. If the eyebrows are raised, the sign becomes WHAT TIME?

Colour and Time and This and That

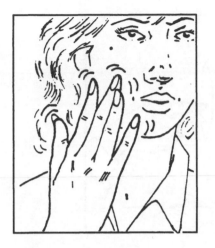

WHEN?
Fingers of open hand flutter against the cheek. **Face and body indicate question form.**

EVERY DAY, DAILY
The backs of the fingers brush forwards across the cheek.

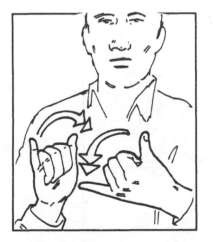

SOMETIMES
Two 'Y' hands, held with palms facing, move from side to side in alternate twisting movements. Also means: SHIFT WORK.

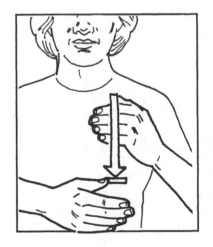

NEVER
R. flat hand chops sharply down the back of palm back L. hand. L. hand may be closed.

Colour and Time and This and That

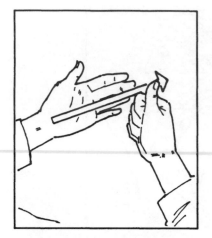

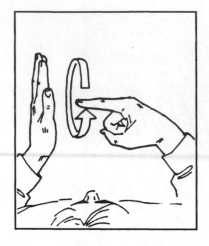

ALWAYS, REGULAR, USUAL
Knuckles of R. closed hand with thumb extended brush forward/right along L. palm.
Variation: knuckles of closed hand brush forward across cheek (regional).

ALL THE TIME
R. index makes repeated forward circular movements pointing towards the L. palm.

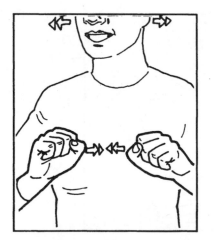

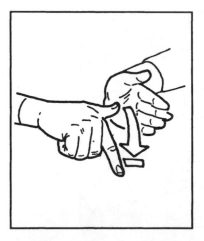

NOT YET
Closed hands, palms forward/down, make several short quick movements towards each other, accompanied by head shake.

LATE
Tip of R. thumb contacts L. palm as R. index twists sharply forward/down. Can be made with index only brushing across L. palm. The index moving forward/right on its own can be used to mean LATER, AFTER

Colour and Time and This and That

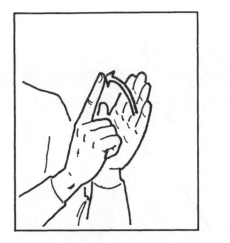

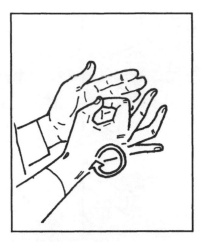

EARLY, EARLIER
Upright R. index finger makes small backward movement on L. palm. **Variation:** blade of R. flat hand contacts back of palm down L. hand and moves backwards in small arc up the left forearm.

HOUR, HOURLY
Tips of R. 'O' hand make forward clockwise circular movement on L. palm. Can be made on the back of L. wrist. Can involve the R. index twisting round in full circle on L. palm or back of wrist.

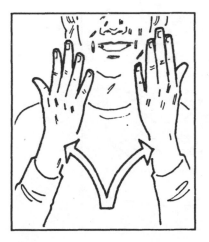

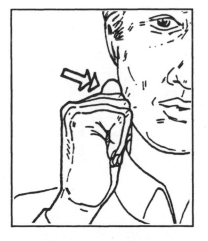

DAY
Palm back flat hands start crossed and swing upwards and apart from the elbows.

DATE
R. closed hand, palm left, taps side of chin twice. Can be made at front of chin and this version also means NUMBER. **Variation:** palm forward R. open hand rests on L. index as the fingers wiggle; this version also means CALENDAR (regional).

Colour and Time and This and That

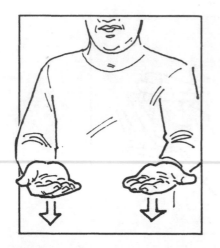

NOW
Flat hands, palms up, move down slightly with stress. If the movement is repeated, the meaning is TODAY. **Variation:** tips of R. bent hand contact L. palm (regional).

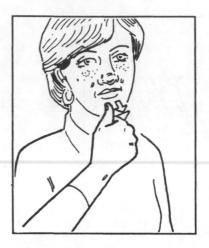

USE, USEFUL
The side of the extended thumb brushes down the chin, twice. **Variation:** tips of palm back bent hand brush down the chin, twice.

LEARN, ABSORB, TAKE IN
Bent hand, with thumb held parallel, moves back towards the side of the head as the fingers close onto the thumb. Can be repeated. Both hands can be used alternately.

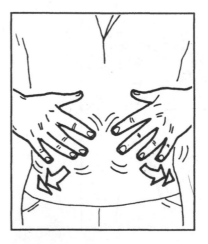

THAT'S ALL!
Palm back open hands shake down/apart twice simultaneously.

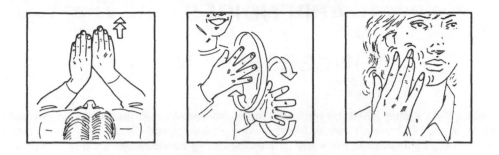

When do you practise signing?

NEVER EVERY DAY LATER
NOT YET SOMETIMES ALL THE TIME
ALWAYS NOW

APPENDICES

FINGERSPELLING

Fingerspelling gives a letter for letter symbolised representation of the written alphabet, formed by the hand or hands. There are many different written alphabets and different forms of manual alphabets in existence throughout the world. Britain uses a two-handed fingerspelling system which originated in the seventeenth century. Irish and American sign languages each have their own one-handed system, as do most of the world's sign languages. The Irish one-handed alphabet is used by some signers in Roman Catholic Deaf communities in various regions of Britain.

The illustrations of fingerspelling shown here are static and two-dimensional, like the sign illustrations, but in normal use they can change form considerably and are best learned in word patterns and rhythms. Although handshapes can be quickly learned, a **lot** of practice is needed to produce and read fluent fingerspelling—BSL users can be very tolerant, but slow and laboured fingerspelling is pure torture (in addition, lip-pattern should reflect words and **not** individual letters, unless they are initials, e.g. BSL).

Fingerspelling is an important and integrated part of BSL, but its frequency of use can vary considerably depending on age, educational background or regional influences, and since it is a representation of English, it should be used with caution. Words may be spelled out in full or contracted, particularly names and places; initialisation is frequently used, or a fingerspelt formation can be incorporated into a sign.

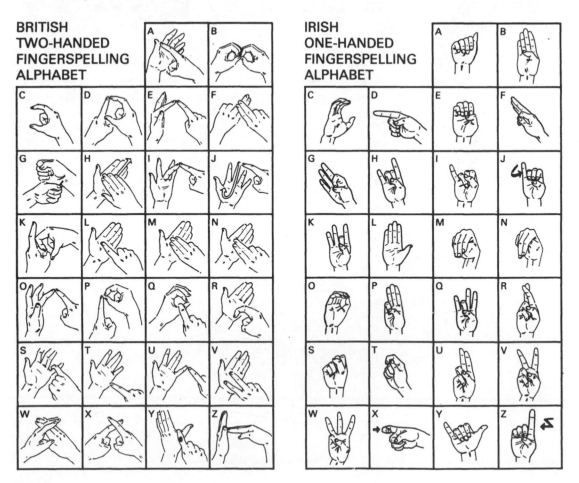

BRITISH TWO-HANDED FINGERSPELLING ALPHABET

IRISH ONE-HANDED FINGERSPELLING ALPHABET

SOURCES AND RECOMMENDED READING

Aichison, J. (February 1996). *The Observer Essay: It ain't what you say . . .* The Sunday Observer Review.

Brennan, M., Colville, M. and Lawson, L. (1984). *Words in Hand: A structural analysis of the signs of British Sign Language*. Edinburgh: Moray House College of Further Education.

British Deaf Association (1992). *Dictionary of British Sign Language/English*. London: Faber and Faber.

Chambers (1990). *Chambers English Dictionary*. Edinburgh: W&R Chambers.

Flodin, M. (1991). *Signing for Kids*. New York: Perigree Books.

Klima, E. and Bellugi, U. (1979). *The Signs of Language*. Harvard University Press.

Rowan, D. (December 1992). *Language*. London: Guardian Newspaper (Education).

Sacks, O. (1990). *Seeing Voices: A journey into the world of the deaf*. London: Pan Books.

Seleskovitch, D. (1978). *Interpreting for International Conferences: Problems of Language and Communication*. Washington, DC: Pen and Booth.

Smith, C. (1990). *Signs Makes Sense: A Guide to British Sign Language*. London: Souvenir Press.

Smith, C. (1992). *Sign in Sight: A Step into the Deaf World*. London: Souvenir Press.

Smith, C. (1999). *Sign Language Link: A pocket dictionary of signs*. Revised edition. Stockton on Tees: Co-Sign Communications.

OTHER SOURCES
OF INFORMATION

Numbers for voice contact are indicated by (V) and for text contact by (T)

British Deaf Association
1–3 Worship Street, London EC2A 2AB. (Tel: 020 7588 3520/3529 (V/T); Fax: 020 7588 3527; http://www.bda.org.uk   e-mail: info@bda.org.uk)

Centre for Deaf Studies
University of Bristol, 8 Woodland Road, Bristol, Avon BS8 1TN. (Tel: 0117 954 6900 (V); 0117 954 6920 (T); Fax: 0117 954 6921)

Council for the Advancement of Communication with Deaf People
Durham University Science Park, Block 4, Stockton Road, Durham DH1 3UZ. (Tel: 0191 383 1155 (V/T); 0191 383 7915 (text answering machine); Fax: 0191 383 7914; http://www.cacdp.demon.co.uk   e-mail: durham@cacdp.co.uk)

Deaf Studies Research Unit
University of Durham, Department of Sociology and Social Policy, Elvet Riverside 2, New Elvet, Durham DH1 3JT. (Tel: 0191 374 2304 (V/T); 0191 374 2314 (T); Fax: 0191 374 4743; e-mail: b.j.clarke@durham.ac.uk)

'Deafview'
Tim Russell, 19–23 Featherstone Street, London EC1Y 8SL. (Tel: 020 7296 8145 (V); Fax: 020 7296 8021)

The Forest Bookshop (Books, Videos, etc. on sign language/deaf issues)
8 St John Street, Coleford, Gloucestershire GL16 8AR. (Tel: 01594 833858 (V/T); Videophone: 01594 810537; Fax: 01594 833446; Web shopping site: www.ForestBooks.com e-mail: deafbooks@forestbooks.com)

LASER: The Language of Sign used as an Educational Resource
c/o 8 Church Lane, Kimpton, Hitchen, Hertfordshire SG4 8RP. (Tel: 01438 832676 (V/T); Fax: 01438 833699   e-mail: laser@adept@nildram.co.uk)

The National Deaf Children's Society
National Office: 15 Dufferin Street, London EC1Y 8PD. (Tel: 020 7250 0123 (V/T); Parents' Helpline 2pm–5pm 0800 252380; Fax: 020 7251 5020   e-mail: ndcs@ndcs.org.uk)

'Read Hear'
Jennifer Dodds, CSV Media, 237 Pentonville Road, London N1 9NJ. (Tel: 020 7833 1894 (T); Fax: 020 7833 5689)

Royal National Institute for Deaf People
19–23 Featherstone Street, London EC1Y 8SL. (Tel: 020 7296 8000 (V); 020 7296 8001 (T); Fax: 020 7296 8199; Helpline: 0870 60 50 123 (V); 0870 60 33 007 (T); http://www.rnid.org.uk   e-mail: helpline@rnid.org.uk)

TYPETALK: National Telephone Relay Service
John Wood House, Glacier Building, Harrington Road, Brunswick Business Park, Liverpool L3 4DF. (Fax: 0151 709 8119; Helpline: 0800 7311 888 (V); 0800 500 888 (T); Relay: 0800 959598 (T); 0800 515152 (V); Emergency Relay: 0800 112 999 (T)   e-mail: helpline@rnid.org.uk)

INDEX